Finer Than Gold
Sweeter Than Honey

is a Path Book
offering practical spirituality
to enrich everyday living

"Your word is a lamp to my feet
and a light to my path."
Psalm 119:105

Finer Than Gold Sweeter Than Honey

The Psalms for Our Living

Herbert O'Driscoll

Path Books
A LIGHT TO MY PATH

ABC Publishing, Anglican Book Centre
General Synod of the Anglican Church of Canada
80 Hayden Street, Toronto, ON, Canada M4Y 3G2
abcpublishing@national.anglican.ca
www.abcpublishing.com www.pathbooks.com

Reflections on the Psalms of David copyright © 2006
   by Herbert O'Driscoll
Suggestions for Reflection and Prayer copyright © 2006
   by Robert Maclennan

Quotations from the Book of Psalms are from *The Book of Alternative Services*, copyright 1985 by the General Synod of the Anglican
Church of Canada.

Cover illustration : "King David the Psalmist," The British Library

Text set in Garamond, Optima, and Iona
Cover and text design by Jane Thornton

Library and Archives Canada Cataloguing in Publication
O'Driscoll, Herbert, 1928-
   Finer than gold, sweeter than honey : the Psalms for our living
/ Herbert O'Driscoll.

ISBN 1-55126-449-8
   1. Bible. O.T. Psalms--Meditations. I. Title.

BS1430.54.O37 2006   223'.206   C2005-906932-5

Printed in Canada

for Paula
with love
in our fiftieth year

The judgements of the Lord are true and righteous altogether.
More to be desired are they than gold,
more than much fine gold,
sweeter far than honey, than honey in the comb.
— Psalm 19:9–10

Introduction

I came to the psalms as a choirboy and a schoolboy. In my memory, a particular room is associated with each experience.

The first is the large high-ceilinged choir room of St. Luke's Church in Cork, Ireland, where Mr. Garrett, short in stature but rich in those gifts needed to be the master of a boys' choir, drilled us weekly in the singing of the psalms. For him the psalm was never merely a bridge to be crossed casually from the Venite to the First Lesson. The psalm would initially be explained, at least its main theme. Then, whatever the mood of the psalm might be—tenderness, rage, praise, awe, adoration—that particular feeling was demanded of our singing, sometimes pursued at the cost of seemingly endless repetition.

The second room is the big parish schoolroom. At least, I remember it as large and even cavernous. During the week, the psalms were part of a rich diet of learning by heart—a tradition that was still very much alive in the Ireland of the nineteen thirties and forties. Along with speeches from Shakespeare, passages from Paul's epistles, prayer book collects, not to mention great prayers (for example, "for all sorts and conditions") and hymns—all were recited from memory, and all became the ingredients of a process of Christian formation absorbed at a level deeper then mere intellectual understanding.

It was quite extraordinary how deeply the landscapes of scripture blended with the surrounding world of everyday perception. The large eyes of the cattle on my grandfather's farm became "great bulls of Bashan come about me." To stand on the beach looking out at the ocean was to hear "there goes that Leviathan," and to imagine great dark shapes in the unseen depths. To watch the sunrise through the small window of my grandfather's bedroom was to be aware of a majesty "which cometh forth…out of his chamber, and rejoiceth as a giant to run his course" (*The Book of Common Prayer*).

Today, in retirement, I find myself as often in a pew as at an altar or in a pulpit. Among my many learnings from the pew is a realization that the psalms, while faithfully sung, are rarely if ever given even the shortest introduction that might help to integrate them into the liturgy; nor are they likely to be a focus of the homily. Consequently, for many people, the psalm tends to stand in isolation from the rest of the liturgy. I sometimes think that, if we were to ask members of a congregation what role the psalm plays in their worship, or what the psalm has communicated to them, many would find it difficult to respond.

Steps are being taken to address this. One will come across various metrical versions of psalms being sung as hymns. There is an increasing use of responsive psalm singing led by a cantor and drawing a response from the congregation. Usually the repeated congregational response serves as a pointer to the overall theme of the psalm.

In no way am I claiming in these pages to define "the meaning" of a psalm. Poetry—and the psalms are among the most sublime poetry in the world—can never have a single meaning. Like all great writing, the psalms are inexhaustible wells of meaning arising out of the ongoing inner conversation between the text and the reader or singer. My purpose in these short reflections is to attempt to convey succinctly a particular spiritual insight, or insights, that I discern in the psalm, to point to particular phrases or images that I think will engage spiritual reflection, and, if the reader so desires, to offer material for homiletical preparation.

At the end of each reflection, thanks to the generous help of my publisher Robert Maclennan, there are suggestions that may make these pages useful for personal reflection, group discussion, and prayer.

It has been said that there are two great elements in literature that have succeeded in expressing every aspect of human experience and the human condition: the plays of Shakespeare and—to use their familiar biblical title—the Psalms of David. To the extent that this statement is true, it gives great pause to anyone who assumes to comment on either! These reflections are offered in full acknowledgement of this daunting reality.

Psalm 1

The Lord knows the way of the righteous,
but the way of the wicked is doomed.

The world of the psalms is one where, most of the time, the modern Western mind can feel at home. All the things of human experience exist somewhere in the psalms. Joy, sadness, fear, anger, terror, depression, hopelessness, trust—all are here. But there are moments when we can be brought up sharply, as we realize that some things in this world of the psalms are not altogether to our liking.

"Happy are they who have not walked in the counsel of the wicked ... The wicked ... are like chaff which the wind blows away ... The Lord knows the way of the righteous." We are immediately in a black and white world. Between the wicked and the righteous there are no gradations. We are either with one or the other.

We find this troubling. We have become loathe to label people with such ease. Defining what is wicked or righteous is more complex for us. We ask to know more. We wish to probe the motivation behind the act, to see its total context, framed by what we know of the person. We may acknowledge a particular action to be wicked but still refuse to apply that label to the person. We see life in shades of grey. The psalms challenge this. "The wicked shall not stand upright when judgement comes."

The gift of this psalm is precisely in its challenge to us. It forces us to dialogue with it. We are a generation affected deeply by the many psychologies of our time, nervous about making what we currently call value judgements. But the end of a terrible century is reminding us of the reality of evil and wickedness, whether personal or corporate.

We are becoming aware that decisions and actions are cumulative, leading us gradually toward what the psalm calls wickedness or righteousness. Repetition will eventually shape us. The psalmist seems to recognize the reality of this process in such phrases as "walked in the counsel of the wicked" or "lingered in the way of sinners."

This psalm probes most deeply into our modern consciousness in the three words "when judgement comes." For the psalmist this is a matter not of "if" but of "when." Already the psalms have jolted us into paying attention.

∽

Recall an action that you could label "bad." What false "good" could the perpetrator(s) have imagined resulting? What genuine good could you imagine resulting, perhaps indirectly? Ask God to inspire all people to seek the will of God in all things.

Psalm 2

Now, you kings, be wise;
be warned, you rulers of the earth.

This is very much a song of its own particular age and society. It is full of self-confidence and a sense of unquestioned self-superiority. We are in the presence of a ruler sitting on his throne. Reports have been brought to him telling of restlessness among those whom he and his country have conquered. These oppressed people see a chance to break free.

"How perfectly ridiculous," our ruler seems to say. "Don't they realize that God is on my side?" "The Lord has them in derision … He speaks to them in his wrath … I myself have set my king upon my holy hill in Zion." The sense of superiority goes further as our ruler professes to hear God say, "I will give you the nations for your inheritance, and the ends of the earth for your possession."

How are we to incorporate this psalm into contemporary society and worship? We are certainly not prepared to affirm the arrogant claims it makes. In this century we have sent armies into battle against such claims. Can we find a warning here?

Perhaps any society that has achieved a measure of empire fails to see when its own policies and actions, begun and carried out with the best of intentions, change into oppression; when certain people are regarded as enemies and subversives if they ask for nothing more than their freedom, whether in political or economic terms.

If we are prepared to sing this psalm in these terms and with this application, then it speaks to us clearly and directly in its last verses. "Be wise, be warned, you rulers of the earth. Submit to the Lord." These words are addressed to all who hold power of any kind. And they are being warned not to make the mistake of seeing themselves as the repository of power.

All seeming authority and power derive from the ultimate source of authority and power—whom the psalmist names "the Lord." In this way the psalm can be ours to sing, and its warning ours to heed.

≈

Recall a time when you may have been oppressed by power and authority. Consider someone you know who is oppressed by power and authority. Ask God to show them a way through their suffering and to soften the hearts of their oppressors.

Psalm 3

You, O Lord, are a shield about me;
you are my glory, the one who lifts up my head.

There is no gradual introduction, no soothing reassurance before we are exposed to the first piercing cry. "Lord, how many adversaries I have!" Suddenly we are in the company of someone who is coming apart in front of us. The terrifying realization has just hit home that there are enemies everywhere, far too many to be dealt with. We hear of "multitudes of people who set themselves against me all around."

As we listen, we realize that this person is on the verge of paranoia. "How many there are who say of me, 'there is no help for him in his God.'" There are voices whispering, sniggering, jeering, taunting, suggesting that all options have run out, that there are no longer any resources available.

Moments such as this reveal for all of us the presence or absence of inner resources. One of the greatest gifts of the Book of Psalms may be that it takes us to such moments of human experience again and again. The psalmist fully shares a sense of desperation, a feeling of not being able to cope. Nothing is held back. As readers, we are allowed into the inner sanctum of a life. We watch someone's agony.

But we also watch as recovery begins, and it comes with the realization of the grace of God. "You, O Lord, are a shield about me ... I wake ... because the Lord sustains me. I do not fear." This realization turns into an almost savage energy. "Strike all my enemies across the face … break the teeth of the wicked." Hearing this may at first appall us. Nowadays we tend not to allow ourselves so free an expression of deep resentment.

Even though the psalms speak to us from a culture that routinely indulges in extreme language, nevertheless we are being pointed to a fundamental truth. To possess a stubborn conviction that God is faithful in every circumstance can make all the difference between personal disintegration and recovery.

The timeless message of this song comes to us strong and clear in its last verse. "Deliverance belongs to the Lord."

≈

Consider a serious frustration in your life. Ask God to show you a way through your trouble. Consider someone you know who is suffering a serious frustration in their life. Ask God to be with them and to show them a way through their suffering.

Psalm 4

Many are saying, "Oh, that we might see better times!"…
You have put gladness in my heart
more than when grain and wine and oil increase.

These days we tend to dialogue a great deal with ourselves—questioning, examining, analyzing, blaming, agonizing. For the psalmist it is more natural to dialogue with God. So when he feels "hard-pressed," and cries out for mercy and for his prayer to be heard, it is the voice of God that responds.

Obviously God is feeling a little out of patience, not only with the psalmist, but with human nature in general! "How long will you worship dumb idols and run after false gods?" God seems to be suggesting that this particular mortal has his values confused, perhaps putting too much emphasis on material things.

The psalmist's response is a hasty and nervous compliment paid to this obviously disgruntled deity. "The Lord does wonders for the faithful." To which God offers a very tart, if not threatening, response. "Tremble then, and do not sin," and suggests that the psalmist go away and do some hard thinking about his conduct. "Speak to your heart in silence upon your bed." By this time we see a rather chastened supplicant.

The psalmist's thinking now takes another direction. "Many are saying, 'Oh, that we might see better times!' " This plea expresses a very understandable and contemporary longing that echoes in almost every corner of our own society. So we need to take note of the psalmist's approach. It begins with a short prayer. "Lift up the light of your countenance upon us, O Lord." This leads to a complete change of tone and attitude, as if the very act of turning to God becomes itself a source of hope and new life.

There is also the realization that what the psalmist really needs is not more material things, but the grace that comes from the presence and power of God to uplift, encourage, and transform. Not only does he cry out, "You have put gladness in my heart," but, as if surprised at his own discovery, he adds "[this gladness] is more than when grain and wine and oil increase."

Perhaps we are being told something that can be expressed in a slight adaptation of a well-known phrase used in political commentary. We often hear or read the trenchant remark, "It's the economy, stupid." It would seem that this psalm is suggesting the very opposite: "It's not the economy, stupid." Beyond economic problems, important though they be, there is a greater issue—our relationship with God.

≈

Consider some material things that your life is strongly built around. How could they possibly be obstructing your relationship with God? How could they possibly serve to enhance your relationship with God? Ask God to inform your mind and heart.

Psalm 5

All who take refuge in you will be glad;
they will sing out their joy for ever.

In his book *From Beirut to Jerusalem,* Thomas Friedman shows why the worlds of the West and the Middle East find it difficult to understand one another. One reason is that, in Middle Eastern life, the quality of forgiveness, or the refusal to act in response to being wronged or offended, can easily be taken for weakness, and can even lead to further attack.

Again and again the psalmist comes before God to plead a case, and the issue is almost always the same. Enemies surround him. He feels that he has done no wrong to deserve this. He beseeches God for help and, in the same breath, calls down the wrath of God on those who afflict him. "Those who lie in wait for me ... there is no truth in their mouth; there is destruction in their heart. Their throat is an open grave ... Declare them guilty, O God."

Encountered repeatedly, this pattern becomes troubling to our modern ears. We begin to ask if perhaps the psalmist is projecting his own faults on to others. But something else in the pattern brings us up short. We find it here in the lines, "You are not a God who takes pleasure in wickedness, and evil cannot dwell with you. Braggarts cannot stand in your sight ... You destroy those who speak lies; the bloodthirsty and the deceitful, O Lord, you abhor."

The reason for the psalmist's intense hatred of all that he regards as evil is not his imagined personal purity, but his blinding vision of the purity of God. Anything that offends this purity also offends the psalmist as a believer in this God. To him the universe makes no sense if God is other than this kind of absolute purity.

For the psalmist, certain things follow from this view. Either one is the friend or the enemy of this God. And the enemy of this God is therefore one's own enemy, toward whom one can hurl every condemnation with a sense of absolute justification. This is the world of the psalmist. It is one in which we can partially but not wholly live. Nevertheless it is a world that has much spiritual insight to give us.

This psalm calls us to come before God, not casually as our Western minds so often do, but with the thought, "I will bow down toward your holy temple in awe of you."

Again, this psalm offers a beautiful and grace-giving promise that we tend to ignore in our frenzied and driven activism: "All who take refuge in you will be glad; they will sing out their joy for ever." These are the gifts of this psalm.

＠

What is your understanding about the nature of God? How committed are you to those virtues that you attribute to God? Ask God for greater understanding and commitment to realize those virtues in your life. Pray that all people may seek the will of God.

psalm 6

The Lord has heard my supplication;
the Lord accepts my prayer.

The more we read the psalms, the more we become aware of their deep intensity. Whether it be joy or fear, depression or anxiety, or any other human emotion, these emotions are never felt mildly in the world of the psalms. Nobody in the psalms ever says, "I feel rather depressed today" or "I'm a little worried about such and such." Instead one cries out, as the psalmist does here, "I drench my bed and flood my couch with tears" or "My spirit shakes with terror."

Unless we remind ourselves of the tendency in Eastern life to use language that to us seems exaggerated, we can be persuaded that these people lived with constant and dreadful intensity and stress. As a consequence, we may find it difficult to identify with the language of the psalms, and they can cease to speak to us about our human condition.

Obviously the psalmist is under great stress and, equally obviously, this has been going on for some time. We hear the cry, "How long, O Lord, how long?" From our own experience we identify with his distress. We know very well that the most steadfast courage can be worn down if there seems no end in sight to what is afflicting us.

We can only guess at the demons the psalmist wrestles with. The language seems to point to a period of actual sickness. "I am weak; heal me, Lord, for my bones are racked." He is beginning to feel the dread that comes over us all when a malady continues and nothing seems to shake it.

Dark fears emerge from within, fears we hesitate even to name. "In death no one remembers you; and who will give you thanks in the grave?" This ultimate fear is forced into words because the psalmist's resistance has been weakened over weeks and months. The cry, "[I am] worn away because of all my enemies," suggests that the pain and sickness are finally threatening life itself.

But, as so often happens in the psalms, giving vent to fears, expressing deepest feelings, has an immediate effect. If we listen again to the verses of this psalm, we hear the word "Lord" ringing through its cadences like a resonant chord, but always in the background. Suddenly this chord assumes dominance and floods the soul with its assurance. "The Lord has heard the sound of my weeping. The Lord has heard my supplication; the Lord accepts my prayer."

And what do we see? Enemies are routed. It is they who now quake. Healing takes place. Life pulses back.

~

Recall a time when you have suffered. Ask God to be with you. Give yourself permission to feel and accept the suffering. Be kind and gentle with yourself. Ask God to feel the depth of your suffering with you. Ask God to be with all who suffer.

Psalm 7

Awake, O my God, decree justice …
O Lord, judge the nations.

Among the many gifts of parenthood—and also grandparent-
hood—is to witness, and to receive the utter trust of, a small child.
We know sadly that the level of trust declines as time goes by, never
entirely disappearing but lessening as life inculcates some wariness
in all of us.

We need this image of early years to comprehend the level of
unwavering trust in God expressed by the psalmist. It is hardly
possible to read the opening line, "O Lord my God, I take refuge
in you," without feeling a trust that is absolutely sure of itself and
holds nothing back. If most of us are honest, we will admit to a
twinge of envy.

But trouble is at hand. The psalmist is not specific. Whatever
has happened, certain relationships have gone wrong. There are
those who wish recompense of some sort, and they are prepared to
be unpleasant in the pursuit of it. Rightly or wrongly the psalm-
ist believes he is innocent: "O Lord my God, if I have done these
things … then let my enemy pursue and overtake me."

But if he is indeed innocent, then he requires not only protec-
tion. He insists on recompense. "Rise up against the fury of my
enemies," he demands of God. "Awake … decree justice … Give
judgement for me … establish the righteous."

We listen in something like awe to this self-assurance. But it
goes even further. Having demanded that God be his protector,

the psalmist now wants God to be his champion. "God will whet his sword; he will bend his bow and make it ready … he makes his arrows shafts of fire."

The psalmist believes that he can expect justice because he is convinced that it is the nature of God to be just and to do justice. "God is a righteous judge; God sits in judgement every day." Consequently, the psalmist believes that he has a right to expect justice in his own experience. He goes further and expects such justice to be the measure of God's dealings with whole societies. "O my God, decree justice … Be seated on your lofty throne … O Lord, judge the nations."

We need to note where, for the psalmist, this sense of self-justification comes from, because it bears a gift for us. We have come far, in our day, from such a deep faith in God, such a great trust in the constancy that gives foundation to human experience and in human affairs. Once again we are in debt to the psalmist.

❦

Compare the qualities of justice that the world accepts, and the qualities of justice that Jesus lived and taught. Which qualities of justice obtain in your society? Ask God to inspire your prayers and guide your actions to bring the justice of Jesus into the world.

Psalm 8

O Lord our governor,
how exalted is your name in all the world!

J. B. Phillips, one of the very gifted Bible translators of the last century, used to insist that our God is too small—meaning, of course, that our concept of God is insufficient. Not so with the psalmist.

Millennia before the first space shuttle blasted off from Cape Canaveral to show us the earth from space, the psalmist conveys a sense of infinite space when he speaks of God. This is not the God of a mere city or a single country. "O Lord our governor, how exalted is your name in all the world!" But even this is not enough. "Your majesty is praised above the heavens."

The psalmist is experiencing one of those moments that come to us all. It may have happened first to us as a child, gazing at the night sky from a country road, the stars blazing as they never do for us in the city. Perhaps it is such a memory from his own childhood that makes the psalmist say, "Out of the mouths of infants and children your majesty is praised."

"When I consider your heavens, the work of your fingers." What a subtle and gracefully paid compliment to the majesty of God. To send the moon and the stars on their heavenly courses requires nothing more than a flick of the divine fingers! No struggle, no challenge—a mere gesture.

Then comes the mysterious question, as it occurs to all of us under the shining canopy of the night sky: What is my place in all of this vastness? "What is man that you should be mindful of him? the son of man that you should seek him out?" The question first sounds inside oneself, but then reaches out to encompass the whole of humanity and the mysterious human story.

And what intrigues the psalmist is the question that has for us become an immense challenge: "You give [human beings] mastery over the works of your hands." Notice the reminder that humanity is not the maker, but merely the recipient of the gift.

And what is the nature of this "mastery" that we have so sadly mishandled and even betrayed? Even as we ask, the psalmist spells out our eternal responsibility. It is nothing less than for "all sheep and oxen, even the wild beasts of the field, The birds of the air, the fish of the sea."

The psalmist's repeated naming of God as governor is a reminder. We will truly govern our dealings with the rest of this planetary creation only when we see ourselves as the creatures of a God who governs us, and who demands that we be accountable for the gift of creation given to us.

❧

Consider some entity that you love in the world of nature—human or animal, tree or flower, mountain or valley, lake or river, field or forest—anything. Ask yourself how God feels toward this entity. Ask God to move all people to love and care for creation.

Psalm 9

The needy shall not always be forgotten,
and the hope of the poor shall not perish for ever.

For the psalmist, the single word that describes our relationship with God is "trust." To those who trust God come resources that can carry them through the most daunting experiences. "You never forsake those who seek you, O Lord."

Obviously, the psalmist himself has endured such experiences. We are spared the exact details, but not knowing makes it easier for us to apply the psalm to our own circumstances. In true psalmist fashion the struggle is between good (his own) and evil (his enemies'). "You have rebuked the ungodly and destroyed the wicked."

An attractive trait in the psalms is the readiness of the psalmist to thank God. We are usually quite ready to implore God for help or guidance or an endless variety of things. We are less ready to give thanks. "I will give thanks to you, O Lord … I will be glad and rejoice in you … I will sing to your name."

Again, because of the unshakeable trust the psalmist has in God, the word "if" is nearly absent from his vocabulary. Almost always we hear the word "when." "When my enemies are driven back." The psalmist is so certain of God's help that he is able to say, "As for the enemy, they are finished." Even more remarkable, he can say this while he is still deeply embroiled in the struggle. "Have pity on me, O Lord; see the misery I suffer from those who hate me."

The psalmist's deep trust does not come from any denial of his situation, but from utter conviction that, even as he thrashes around in his continuing struggles with life, there is One he knows who will "lift me up from the gate of death."

As always, the source of this trust lies in what the psalmist understands to be the nature of God. Because "the Lord is known by his acts of justice," then somehow, in spite of everything, justice will emerge in our dealings with life. For the psalmist this is particularly true where there is oppression with injustice. "The Lord will be a refuge for the oppressed … The needy shall not always be forgotten, and the hope of the poor shall not perish for ever."

These verses have rung down through the ages, offering hope and changing lives.

❧

Consider someone you trust implicitly. What characteristics in them elicit your trust? How do you behave in the presence of, or in response to, this person? Could you behave this way in your relationship with God? Ask God to strengthen your trust.

Psalm 10

The Lord is king for ever and ever …
To give justice to the orphan and oppressed.

"Why do you stand so far off, O Lord, and hide yourself in time of trouble?" This cry echoes down through time, in every generation. At certain moments in life the question is voiced by all of us.

It would seem that cry of the psalmist is not linked to any present personal agony. Instead it issues from a condition he regards as rampant in his society. "The wicked arrogantly persecute the poor … They lurk in ambush in public squares … they murder the innocent; they spy out the helpless."

But there is something beyond all this that troubles the psalmist at least as much. It is the attitude of those who perpetrate such crimes. "The wicked are so proud that they care not for God; their only thought is, 'God does not matter' … They say in their heart, 'God has forgotten.' "

Most of us are painfully aware that almost all the psalmist's images point to a similar condition in our own society. For us, the phrases "lurk in public squares" and "murder the innocent" appear too often in the daily news, and are becoming so familiar that they seldom merit headlines. In our day, people of power and authority too often "persecute the poor" in the name of such apparently desirable goals as the restructuring of society or the new corporate agenda.

But beyond the ghastliness of crime and the brutalities of what we call the market economy, there is an even more troubling question for us today. While much in our society remains fine and worthy of loyalty, people increasingly live on the assumption that "God does not matter," that human actions and policies need no transcendent source to guide or nourish or judge them. "They say in their heart, 'I shall not be shaken … God has forgotten.' "

For the psalmist, the blemishes of his society are unacceptable. If "the Lord is king," then there must be "justice to the orphan and oppressed." For him, it is inconceivable to think otherwise.

Centuries later a young woman who is poor—both she and her child are in great danger from the awful powers of her society—recalls such a song as this. She prays for justice in the world and safety for her child. "He has cast down the mighty from their thrones," sings Mary, "and has lifted up the lowly."

❧

Consider a person or group who suffer cruelty and oppression. Ask God to be with them and to give them courage and comfort. Ask God to be with their oppressors, to show them the suffering they cause, and to move them to deeds of compassion.

Psalm 11

In the Lord have I taken refuge;
how then can you say to me,
"Fly away like a bird to the hilltop."

Thomas Merton, the Trappist monk whose writings became a major part of twentieth-century Christian life, spent the first half of his ordained life in the seclusion and detachment of Gethsemane Abbey. Though he did not often leave the abbey, he spent the second half of his life in passionate involvement in the divisive issues of American society during the nineteen sixties and seventies.

At the point of change in his stance, Merton wrote a book whose title explains his change of attitude. He called the book *Conjectures of a Guilty Bystander.*

Merton's change of attitude would be understood by the psalmist. Obviously, things are seriously wrong in his society. We are not given specifics, but we can surmise what is adrift. "The wicked ... ambush ... the true of heart." It is becoming difficult to live a life of integrity. There is a reference to "those who delight in violence," one of the sure signs of a troubled society. Most ominous, there seems to be some justification for saying that "the foundations are being destroyed."

Much of what goes on in our own time allows us to identify with the thoughts and feelings of the psalmist—especially when we must choose a response to what is happening around us. The psalmist expresses the dilemma. "When the foundations are being destroyed, what can the righteous do?" For the psalmist, one of two courses seems possible. We can, as many advise, try to opt out and "fly away like a bird to the hilltop"—assuming we have the means and the opportunity.

But if we are people of faith, who try to base our actions and choices on trust in a righteous God, there is the certainty that our lives and actions are both observed and judged. "[The Lord's] eyes behold the inhabited world." Even more sobering is the knowledge that "[the Lord's] piercing eye weighs our worth."

For the psalmist, the choice is to reject escapism and accept action and service. "In the Lord have I taken refuge." Whatever contribution can be made, the psalmist will make it, because "[the Lord] delights in righteous deeds."

&

Is there an evil in your society or the world that particularly troubles you? Ask God what you could reasonably do to help alleviate or eradicate it. Remember that frequent and regular prayer for others, in the light of God's presence, is a sacred act of charity.

Psalm 12

"Because the needy are oppressed ...
I will rise up," says the Lord,
and give them the help they long for."

There are moments when Winston Smith, the central character in George Orwell's *Nineteen Eighty-Four*, seems to appear between the lines of the psalms, particularly as the psalmist agonizes about the state of his society. There is the same sense of alienation from those around him, as well as from the social structures. There is a feeling of loneliness, sometimes of fear.

The great difference between the two is that, for the psalmist, there is the presence of God giving meaning to everything, while for Smith, there is nothing above and beyond what is, or what seems to be.

As a person of faith, even though he is moving among people who consider themselves to be the people of God, the psalmist feels alone. "There is no godly one left; the faithful have vanished." Trust has been drained away: "Everyone speaks falsely." What is harder to accept is the way that speech has been used to deceive: "With a smooth tongue they speak from a double heart." The vehemence with which the psalmist rails against the corruption of speech suggests that he himself has been deceived.

We can't help being reminded of the use of language in our own time, much of it expressly designed to manipulate and seduce. The managing of news media, and the ever-increasing skills of marketing, come easily to mind. Whatever the particular deceptions being practised in the psalmist's society, it is obvious that at least one objective is economic deprivation. "The needy are oppressed, and the poor cry out in misery."

At this point the psalmist becomes much more than someone who merely laments a state of affairs. Suddenly he voices the certainty that these evils will be corrected and suffering will be relieved. " 'I will rise up,' says the Lord, 'and give them the help they long for.' " For the psalmist, God is always the moral power from which justice flows.

Again the psalmist focuses on language to make his point. He contrasts the "smooth tongues" of those around him with the "pure words" of the Lord, "purified seven times in the fire." In the face of declining standards all around him, where "that which is worthless is highly prized," he offers the infinite worth of God, whose words are "like silver refined from ore."

Once again, as in many of the psalms, the singer is appalled by contemporary events, but is never without a stubborn hope.

❧

Can you discern occasions of duplicity in the voices of your society and yourself? Ask God to nurture, in you and others, perceptive minds and hearts to discern duplicity in the world and themselves, and to seek conscientiously for honesty, truth, and grace.

Psalm 13

How long, O Lord?
will you forget me for ever?

This is a song that begins in anguish and ends, almost unbelievably, in joy. It is almost impossible to read the opening verses without being reminded of Hamlet's agonized cry on the battlements of Elsinore: "O, that this too too solid flesh would melt, thaw and resolve itself into a dew!"

"How long, O Lord?" Since the human voice found words to express human feelings, this cry has gone up to the gods. We can withstand so much—so much pain, so much hatred, so much aggression against us—but there comes a time when resistance is ground down and our resources are exhausted. We can feel control slipping.

Our response is even more compromised by a haunting fear that all our troubles transpire in an utterly uncaring universe. Even the person of faith—which the psalmist certainly is—can dread that God has forgotten his or her very existence. The question, "Will you forget me for ever?" is poignant beyond words.

But perhaps, for the person of faith, there is an even greater terror than the fear of being forgotten by God. We can entertain the suspicion that God is playing a merciless cat and mouse game with our life and its pain, that God is hiding, inviting a fruitless search to which God may, or may not, whimsically respond. All this agony rings out in the cry, "How long will you hide your face from me?"

Both the mental and emotional faculties of the psalmist are being stressed to the breaking point. "How long shall I have perplexity in my mind, and grief in my heart?" So often we hear someone cry out that they think their mind is going. "How long shall my enemy triumph over me?" There is a feeling of utter defeat coupled with a desperate plea for help: "Look upon me ... give light to my eyes, lest I sleep in death."

But now we begin to hear, once again, the glory that is everywhere in the psalms—quite literally, the glory of God. Nothing can displace the profound faith of the psalmist: "I [will] put my trust in your mercy." The first springtime of joy comes in the wintertime of despair: "My heart is joyful ... I will sing ... I will praise the name of the Lord Most High."

We are watching as someone snatches true victory from apparent defeat, and we pray that this may be so in our experience also.

❦

Have you suffered despair? Do you know someone who suffers despair? Ask God to embrace those in despair with the divine presence, to give them compassion for themselves and others in despair, and to illuminate them with the light of grace.

Psalm 14

When the Lord restores the fortunes of his people,
Jacob will rejoice and Israel be glad.

As one stands by the Wailing Wall in Jerusalem and watches men and women praying fervently, it is easy to forget that much of their prayer is for those around them who do not profess faith, at least in any religious sense. The prayer of the faithful is offered for the recovery of faith among the majority of Israelis who live from a secular stance.

Sometimes when we read the psalms, we encounter statements that seem to contradict all our assumptions about the world from which they come. We assume that the psalmist speaks from an age and society of faith, and so we can often be astonished at his distress about the state of religious faith and practice around him.

His lament has a very modern sound. We ourselves can easily identify with the statement, "There is no God"—our culture is actually based on this assumption. Unbelief is so common in our society that it no longer produces any sense of shock or surprise.

But there is something we need to notice about the psalmist's claim. He links the loss of faith in God to the overall deterioration of his society. The statement, "There is no God," is immediately followed by the assertion that society is inherently "corrupt"—"every one has proved faithless" and "there is none who does any good."

The psalmist is free with generalities. In condemning his society he is quite ready to say that "all alike have turned bad." We rightly question such sweeping statements. Even in the most corrupt societies there are men and women who strive to live lives of integrity, often at great cost. Although their integrity may not derive from their religious stance, this does not mean that we can discount the integrity itself.

In all fairness to the psalmist, he moves from condemnation to hope before he ends his song. It is not a case of "if the Lord" but "when the Lord restores the fortunes of his people." The same hopeful stance is required of us, even more so when we are tempted to see growing moral decay in our own society, or when we feel that its social fabric is weakening.

Instead of giving up on our society and dismissing it, we are called increasingly to fervent prayer that God's infinite power to restore may become more and more evident.

❧

Are there aspects of your society or world society that you would call "corrupt"? Ask yourself why such corruption occurs. Ask God to guide all people in the pursuit of generosity, honesty, and justice, and to inspire them with hope for a just society.

Psalm 15

Lord, who may dwell in your tabernacle?
who may abide upon your holy hill?

To read this psalm is to find oneself recalling George Herbert's poem entitled "Love." As well as being a beautiful piece of English poetry, it is also a magnificent spiritual statement. "Love bade me welcome," writes Herbert, "yet my soul drew back, guiltie of dust and sinne."

The dialogue between the guest and Love himself continues until the diffident guest is persuaded to accept Love's insistent invitation. The guest feels he is not worthy. For Love this is irrelevant. "You must sit down, sayes Love, and taste my meat." If this psalm does indeed bring Herbert's poem to mind, it may be because of the way the poet challenges the theme of this psalm.

The psalmist stands with me before God's "holy hill." I hear the conditions that must be met if I am to reach the tabernacle of God. But as soon as I hear the conditions, I am already defeated! "Whoever leads a blameless life and does what is right." Blameless! Always? Doing what is right! Always? I am tempted to turn away in frustration from the upward path.

The other conditions are equally uncompromising. "No guile upon his tongue." Never a slanting of the truth to allow me to survive in some situation? "No evil to his friend." What of the many hurts I have received, even if unintentional? "In his sight the wicked is rejected, but he honours those who fear the Lord." Is it so easy to divide our world into the wicked and the good, oneself always numbered among the good?

There are more conditions, but already there are too many. As I walk away from this impossible "hill," I hear a final assurance given with the best of intentions: "Whoever does these things shall never be overthrown." But I cannot do all these things. I am already overthrown, and I walk away.

Because I long for God, as does every human being, I turn and gaze sadly back at the mountain. As I look, I see a figure walking down, beckoning to me as Love beckons to the guest in Herbert's poem. I respond to the gesture and return to the upward path.

Now the invitation is given again, but in a different way. I must still climb if I wish to stand in a holy place, but now I can climb with a companion, one who has done what I cannot do—live blamelessly in this world. I do not have to pretend to be more than I truly am. I have neither to boast of my qualities nor apologize for my shortcomings.

I am accepted in this once unattainable high place, not for my worth but for the incomparable worth of Jesus, who is both companion and Lord.

꒰꒱

Are there things you have achieved in life, or personal qualities you have developed, that please you? Make a list of them. Thank God for all the good people and things in your life. Ask God to comfort and support those who feel undeserving and unworthy.

Psalm 16

O Lord, you are my portion and my cup;
it is you who uphold my lot.

We live in a culture that mistrusts value judgements. If at all possible, we try to avoid making them. Such an attitude is utterly irreconcilable with the world of the psalms.

In our culture, to say, "All my delight is upon the godly" and the "noble among the people," commending those who are committed to the same concept of God as myself, may be barely acceptable. But to dismiss those who have chosen otherwise, and aspire to "run after other gods," is quite unacceptable unless we are prepared to enter a world of fundamentalist religious stance.

To go even further, to promise trouble for those who differ from us in matters of religious faith, to say that they "shall have their troubles multiplied," puts us outside the bounds of moral behaviour.

Beyond these opening verses the psalm has much that we can heartily agree to. For us, God can indeed be "my portion and my cup," the source of nourishment and satisfaction for the hunger and thirst of our spirits.

It is indeed God who sustains us in the stresses and challenges of daily living, "who uphold[s] my lot." It is indeed the Holy Spirit of God who makes us aware of blessings already received, and helps us to appreciate the ways that life can sometimes be "a pleasant land" and "a goodly heritage." It is indeed God who can be our source of guidance, "who gives me counsel."

Notice how the psalmist roams through three levels of human experience and claims that God brings grace into all of them. First he maintains that the "heart teaches me, night after night." We know the truth of this. It is often during our night musings that we come to see things with a clarity that eludes us in the day's busyness.

Then there is the claim that, to sense the presence of God in our ongoing activities—that God is "at my right hand"—helps us to stand firm in the face of what life can bring. We will be given courage and stamina to persevere.

Finally the psalmist dares to claim the ultimate. He trusts that the presence of God will be with us at the moment of death itself, and even beyond death. "You will not abandon me to the grave." The psalm ends with a lovely, almost extravagant expectation of "the path of life … fullness of joy … pleasures for evermore." With God we will know ultimate fulfillment.

✑

Every day things happen to make you happy or sad. Every day decisions need to be made. Consider sharing happenings with God, and checking decisions with God, in daily conversation. Continually enter God's presence and listen for God's guidance.

Psalm 17

Keep me as the apple of your eye;
hide me under the shadow of your wings.

As we read some of the psalms, we find ourselves searching for a contemporary equivalent to the world in which the psalmist lives. His society is one where stark lines are drawn. The psalmist feels there are those who are for him and those who are implacably against him. We search in vain for any middle ground.

For the psalmist there are "his people" and "the others." For those others, no word or phrase is too harsh. They are "the wicked who assault me." They are "deadly enemies who surround me." They speak "proud things." (We can assume that "proud" means arrogant.) They are "greedy for … prey," and they are "lurking in secret places." Their "portion in life [all they think about] is this world."

Allowing for the fact that not one of us is without those who dislike us, sometimes intensely; allowing that everyone of us may sometimes have bitter rivals, even enemies—it remains true that there are few times in life when we would be prepared to describe our situation in the siege terms the psalmist uses.

One cannot help but detect a strong streak of envy against those who have obviously prospered. Are these people unscrupulous, and do they therefore merit the psalmist's condemnation? Is their prospering and having children and leaving them well off reprehensible in itself (verse 15)?

Are we listening to a personality who needs to project a dark shadow on to others, so that he himself can be one whose prayer "does not come from lying lips," who offers a confident "plea of innocence" and can say "I give no offence with my mouth as others do; I have heeded the words of [God's] lips?"

In this psalm we may be hearing a self-justifying approach to God, the kind that Jesus sternly dismisses in his parable of the two people in the temple. One person informs God of his utter righteousness when compared with others; the other person offers himself without the least illusion about the poverty of his spiritual state.

Our Lord makes it quite clear that a simple plea for acceptance and forgiveness is infinitely superior to a recital of the sins of those around us.

≈

We are often tempted to blame our unpleasant experiences on others. In the event, we need to ask ourselves if we are entirely without fault. Ask God to help us be honest with ourselves, understanding toward others, and courageous in the face of evil.

Psalm 18

With the help of my God
I will scale any wall.

In the culture of the psalms—as in the Middle East today—nothing is experienced in moderation. Joy is ecstatic, hatred is implacable, love is deep devotion, betrayal is devastating, insults are laden with invective, friendship—while it lasts—is utterly binding.

Relationship with God is given the same extravagant expression. No statement of faith is sufficient without repeated images to describe and emphasize it. For the psalmist, God is "my stronghold, my crag, and my haven ... my shield ... my salvation, and my refuge."

The effects of personal crisis extend far beyond individual experience. Whatever trouble the psalmist has endured assumes cosmic proportions. "Mountains shook ... [God] parted the heavens and came down ... The beds of the seas were uncovered, and the foundations of the world laid bare." In all this upheaval the psalmist stands serenely at the centre, utterly sure of his relationship with God.

How are we to identify with this total moral conviction? Should we envy it or be repelled by it? Perhaps there is another possible response. We can note the massive foundation of trust that sustains the faith of the psalmist. Having indulged in our envy, we cannot but long for this kind of certainty ourselves.

We cannot help but long for the ability to say of God, "You are my lamp ... you make my darkness bright." Even to hear the psalmist say, "with the help of my God I will scale any wall," is to feel one's own faltering resolve strengthened. When we recognize God as the one "who girds me about with strength … makes me sure-footed like a deer and lets me stand firm on the heights," we cannot but feel a surge of confidence and energy within ourselves.

Through such ardent expressions of trust, the psalmist is transformed before us into a warrior able to battle any foe. If these same images can make it possible for us too to cope with life, to conquer the enemies both within and beyond ourselves, then this psalm will become grace for us.

※

Trusting friendships are built in subtle ways, often over long times, and result from deep knowing. How much time do you spend with God? How well do you feel you know God? Consider devoting daily time to being with God and consulting God.

Psalm 19

The heavens declare the glory of God …
The law of the Lord is perfect and revives the soul.

In the desert, the degree to which the sun dictates human activity is a measure of its majesty. One must travel before it rises. One must rest when it blazes down at noon.

"Like a bridegroom out of his chamber," says the psalmist, his eyes squinting as they turn to the golden line of the eastern horizon. "Like a champion to run its course," he muses, as the fire of a new day spills above the horizon and pierces his eyes. Later in the day, his body wracked by heat and sweat, he will murmur through parched lips, "Nothing is hidden from its burning heat."

Now he links the glory of the heavens to the glory of moral law, "the law of the Lord." Images tumble into his mind. There is a terrible perfection about the law, just as there is about the heavens. To contemplate either "revives the soul." To contemplate the skies—day or night—is to feel ourselves as children before an inexpressible mystery. A timeless wisdom is given even to a child, as he or she gazes up. So, with the law of God, there comes mystery and wisdom.

The sun brings the gift of daylight, and we once again can see. So the law of the Lord gives clarity in our search for direction. The sun cleans the desert as a furnace removes refuse. So the law of God cleanses the soul, sometimes with a discipline as pitiless as the sun. The psalmist dwells on this. "Cleanse me from my secret faults," he asks, considering those repressed flaws that not even he is aware of.

So, in the mind of the psalmist, the sun and the heavens become a metaphor for the mystery of God and the demands of God on our humanity. The search for metaphors of God will take each one of us in different directions. For some, it may be the canvasses of great art that trigger insights about God. For others, it may be great music. For still others, it may be a liturgical moment when bread becomes more than bread, and wine more than wine.

All of these, and many other things, are capable of becoming for us what the sun and the heavens are for the psalmist. The nature of the metaphor is not important. What matters is that we develop the ability to think in such a way: to look not merely at the world of daily experience but through it and, looking through it, to see the God who blazes at its centre—its true sun.

The question for each of us can be put in terms of the opening verses of this psalm: What for me declares the glory of God? What for me shows God's handiwork?

❧

Since all creation finds its source in God, all created things reflect the mind and heart of God. Recall and savour the wonderful things in life that thrill you most. May your love of God's creation lead you to ever deeper and fuller relationship with God.

Psalm 20

Some put their trust in chariots and some in horses,
but we will call upon the name of the Lord our God.

At first reading, these lines seem almost out of character for the psalmist. The atmosphere is calm. For once, no enemy is at the gates. We have nothing but unqualified approval for another, as if a dear friend or loved one is being addressed. There is not a word of criticism, no fault finding.

Good wishes for the recipient of this psalm follow each other in quick succession. "May the Lord answer you in the day of trouble … Send you help from his holy place … strengthen you." May God "accept your burnt sacrifice … Grant you your heart's desire … prosper all your plans."

Only now (verse 6) do we realize that the psalmist is writing a somewhat political document. This fervent endorsement is for a leader—a king. Presumably there is some threat of trouble, the possibility of attack or invasion. It would seem that the king is preparing to respond. As he does, his loyal subjects—the psalmist among them—dutifully assure themselves and their king that nothing other than victory is possible.

How does a long-ago statement of political loyalty become a resource for our Christian devotions? Perhaps by our first asking ourselves a question. Who for us is king? For a Christian there can be only one reply. Jesus Christ is king. How do we affirm him as king for us? By generously and genuinely offering our worship and praise, and by committing all aspects of our lives that flow naturally from the loyalty we profess.

There is an echo of this psalm in one of the loveliest of all Christian hymns: "My Song Is Love Unknown," written by Samuel Crossman in the late seventeenth century. "Here might I stay and sing ... never was love, dear King, never was grief like thine." Here is all the same admiration and devotion, but now offered not to an earthly ruler preparing for war, but in gratitude to a king who has won a victory for us at ultimate cost to himself.

Because of our Lord's victory, we can expect to realize some of our own victories in the ongoing struggle with our human nature.

∾

Consider Christ—human and divine—a faultless holy person submitting to humiliation, suffering, and death. Ask God to give you gratitude to Christ for his life and work, and courage to express "Christ in you" (as St. Paul taught), to be a light in the world.

psalm 21

The king puts his trust in the Lord;
because of the loving-kindness of the Most High,
he will not fall.

Near the climax of the process that brought about the resignation of Richard Nixon, the American president went on television flanked by a large and prominent presidential seal. In his speech he implied that, if his honour were impugned, the presidency itself would be irreparably damaged.

The office may well have been damaged but, it would seem, not irreparably so. At the time, great fears were expressed about this possibility. Perhaps the reason why the presidency as an institution proved so resilient lies far back in time and may even be expressed in this psalm.

The psalm begins with what at first glance is a seemingly endless succession of sycophantic praises of those in power at the time. The singer offers what he knows will please the royal ears. There will be, and already are, "blessings of prosperity." The ruler's "honour is great." He appears with "splendour and majesty." Here is a polished palace courtier, a singer bound for high places through assured and well-earned royal patronage.

A more careful reading, however, shows us a different reality. The psalm does begin with a direct focus on the person of the king, but in almost every verse the focus swings to God. The king rejoices and exults, not in his own victory but that of God.

God is the source of the "heart's desire" of the king. His

blessings and his crown are the gift of God. Any future victories will depend on the king's "trust in the Lord." The verses toward the end of the psalm begin with "you" and "your," each time referring to God. In the last poetic flourish, it is not the king who is to be exalted, but the Lord.

That now historical day, when a president tried to equate his personal worth with the honour of a great office, showed us a truth. It is often forgotten that both those who bear great office, and the office itself, issue from a source beyond themselves. Both are "under God."

We who are far from being powerful kings and rulers know that this is true of our own lives. All we do and everything we are is "under God." This is the great reality that gives meaning and purpose to our lives. Thanks be to God.

≈

Recall the goodness of nature—land, water, plants, animals. Recall the wonder of the universe—matter, energy, light, consciousness. Recall the love of people—family, friends, associates, others. Pray that you, and all people, may seek and find God in all creation.

Psalm 22

My God, my God, why have you forsaken me? …
Yet you are the Holy One …
kingship belongs to the Lord.

Every great artist's collection includes those "giants" of creation that stand above the rest. For Shakespeare it may be Hamlet; for Michelangelo, the ceiling of the Sistine Chapel. Among the psalms, this song stands out. There are few evocations of human desolation equal to it.

For a Christian, the first line pierces deeply because we hear it also from the lips of our Lord on the cross. "My God, my God, why have you forsaken me?" Some maintain that Jesus may have been turning to this psalm to find some meaning in the agony of crucifixion. But the psalm is not about the crucifixion of our Lord.

The psalmist is writing from a personal agony. Obviously, it has been going on for some time. "I cry in the daytime, but you do not answer; by night as well, but I find no rest." He tries the devices we all know in suffering. God has helped in the past; therefore, the same help should be extended in the present. "Our forefathers … trusted, and you delivered them."

For a moment this thought gives the psalmist some relief, but then there sweeps over him the contempt and dismissal he receives from others. "All who see me laugh me to scorn." A most cruel cost of great suffering is the fear that we are utterly worthless and have become of no consequence, even to friends. "I am a worm and no man, scorned by all."

Once again there is an effort to regain control over his feelings. After all, God is his creator. Surely this suffering is of concern to the creator of his body and soul! "You are he who took me out of the womb." But his effort at control is also swept away in a sudden flood of misery. "I am poured out like water ... my bones are out of joint; my heart within my breast is melting ... My mouth is dried ... dogs close me in ... evildoers circle around me."

Promises are made—the bargaining with God we all know. "I will declare your name ... in the midst of the congregation I will praise you ... I will perform my vows."

Now it seems as if the sufferer has succeeded in handing the pain over to greater hands. "Kingship belongs to the Lord." We may be hearing the voice of someone who is preparing for final surrender. "To him alone all who sleep in the earth bow down." But in the surrender, we receive a vision of hope. "My soul shall live for him."

In these lines we have been given a sublime expression of the determination of the human spirit to find in God meaning and hope in human suffering. May we also discover this grace.

∽

Bring to mind the suffering of people in some area of the world, in your society. Bring to mind the suffering of a friend, your own suffering. Ask God to be with those who suffer and to give them understanding and comfort, healing and grace.

Psalm 23

Surely your goodness and mercy
shall follow me all the days of my life,
and I will dwell in the house of the Lord for ever.

The Wadi Kelt is a deep valley with precipitous sides that runs from a point north-east of Jerusalem, cuts through the edge of the escarpment, and opens out on to the floor of the Jordan valley. Because of its depth, Wadi Kelt loses the evening sun early and fills with shadows.

Most guides will at some time point into the shadows and remind people of the psalm verse where the poet says, "Though I walk through the valley of the shadow of death, I shall fear no evil; for you are with me." It is a tribute to the greatness of this psalm that, centuries later, people feel impelled to give the image an actual geography, even though imaginary.

In the time of our Lord, shepherding was low on the scale of occupations. Shepherds were sought when a dangerous and lonely job needed doing, and they paid a price. For the most part they were looked on as misfits and loners. They moved on the edge of society, were usually mistrusted, and sometimes—probably because of their toughness—were feared. As with Samaritans, prostitutes, and tax gatherers, Jesus identified himself with shepherds, enhancing their role by giving it an image of caring and responsibility.

Commenting on this psalm is rather like reviewing the *Mona Lisa* or *La Pieta* or any other great work of art. The images speak for themselves across culture and time. They, and the form in which they are expressed, speak directly to the human heart.

The language of this psalm carries a healing and reassuring quality. "The Lord ... makes me lie down ... leads me ... revives my soul ... guides me ... comfort[s] me." Each of these phrases responds to a deep human need. The weary are promised rest, the lost are assured of guidance, the depressed are offered revival of the spirit, the hurt are given comfort. Every word calms the mind and soothes the spirit.

As if these things were not enough, the psalm now presents images of welcome and hospitality. "You are with me ... You spread a table before me ... you have anointed my head ... my cup is running over." Hope and confidence return. "Surely your goodness and mercy shall follow me all the days of my life."

The traveller has come home. It is once again possible to engage life.

~

Recall an occasion when you experienced some trouble. Ask God to be with you. Share the anxiety with God. Recall a current trouble. Share the anxiety with God. Rest in God's presence. Now thank God for sharing with you and supporting you.

Psalm 24

Who can ascend the hill of the Lord? …
Those who have clean hands and a pure heart.

Even after fifteen-hundred years, it is moving to stand in the area of Tara in County Meath in Ireland, and to realize that the palace of the high king once stood here overlooking the surrounding plain. In those days our eyes would have gazed out over a vast forest. The person who stood here long ago held power over everything he could see.

The psalmist gives us a similar image of God. But this time we are looking not over a small island kingdom, but across the planet. We are celebrating infinite power.

The psalmist now asks the question, "Who can ascend the hill of the Lord?" How can we experience the presence of God? What serves us best, if we would feel the power of God in our lives? The reply brings us up short. Power as our society thinks of it has no bearing on this matter. When asked to imagine who can stand on the high place with God, we instinctively think of human beings larger than life—powerful, courageous, strong, invulnerable. But our images are swept away as utterly mistaken.

We are given a markedly different set of standards for those who would be the companions of God. "Clean hands and a pure heart … not pledged … to falsehood [or] fraud." We are being told that the criteria necessary for a relationship with God are essentially moral.

To extend these criteria into the realm of society is very much in keeping with the world of the psalms, where personal and communal life are constantly being linked. We live at a time when Western society as a whole is wrestling with the problem of morality, both public and private. On what grounds can moral stances be justified, especially in an increasingly plural society? "Who can stand?" asks the psalmist. Our question is rather, "On what can we stand?"

If we as a society are to "receive a blessing from the Lord"—to become a desirable, peaceful, and just society in which human beings can live creatively and happily—we know that we must find some acceptable moral ground. Without this we will weaken. But with it we will be powerful in the truest and most lasting sense.

✍

Are there some issues of social morality that concern you? Recall how Jesus responded to moral issues. Consider his teachings— Two Great Commandments, Sermon on the Mount, Lord's Prayer, Parables. Ask God to guide your discernment and compassion.

Psalm 25

Protect my life and deliver me;
let me not be put to shame, for I have trusted in you.

Anyone who has the least experience of counselling others knows that it usually takes some time for a person to confide the real agenda they bring to an encounter. There are exceptions, of course. There are times when someone will sit down and pour out what they must share. But most of us will talk first about less intense things, and move only gradually to the real agenda.

The psalmist meets us in this way. At first his topics are safe and unthreatening. "My God, I put my trust in you ... teach me your paths." But there are hints that other matters are not so easy to mention. "Let me not be humiliated ... let the treacherous be disappointed." Now we hear a little more about his relationship with God, his certainty of God's "compassion and love."

Once again he switches theme; this time he refers to "the sins of my youth." But quickly he veers away from this troubling subject and returns to praising God. "Gracious and upright is the Lord ... All the paths of the Lord are love and faithfulness." Suddenly there is an intense appeal. "O Lord, forgive my sin, for it is great." This is followed, as we have come to expect, by more a fervent reflection on God as friend and guide.

Now comes the full flood of the psalmist's suffering. He is "alone and in misery. The sorrows of [his] heart have increased." Again we hear the word "misery." He has enemies. "They bear a violent hatred against me." This time his thoughts about God are very far from calm reflection, and there is a naked appeal for help. "Protect my life ... let me not be put to shame ... my hope has been in you."

The gift of the psalms to us is their honesty about human nature. This one example shows clearly why the whole Book of Psalms has become precious in our heritage. In this psalm the pretending, the struggle to face certain realities, the defences erected before suddenly tumbling down—all are well known to us. We have all known such struggle before finally confessing the truth to ourselves, often finding this truth extremely difficult to face.

Our prayer for such times is that we have One to turn to, of whom we can say, "My hope has been in you ... deliver me ... for I have trusted in you."

~

We can all remember when, because of some perceived fault, we have felt despondent and unworthy. The Book of Genesis says we are made in the image of God. St. Paul speaks of the Christ within. Ask God to help you realize the divine goodness in you.

Psalm 26

My foot stands on level ground;
in the full assembly I will bless the Lord.

I recall a senior executive once saying to me that, at certain times during worship in her parish church, she would become aware of her professional world and of its dissimilarity from the world in which she was standing. Sometimes she wondered if she could continue to bridge these two worlds. She was sure that she could not function without a community of faith and worship to turn to.

To some extent, I think we meet that person in this psalm. In the mind of the psalmist two worlds seem to be clashing. There is an indication that he is preparing to go to the temple for worship. "I will wash my hands in innocence, O Lord, that I may go in procession round your altar." Is there a note of wistfulness as he sees himself, "singing aloud ... and recounting all [God's] wonderful deeds"? Perhaps there is a note of longing in the line, "Lord, I love the house in which you dwell."

This wistfulness and longing may arise from the way that images of the house and presence of God are suddenly juxtaposed with invading images of a brutal world. In the teeth of this world the psalmist is trying to hold on to the things he values. The opening verses have a kind of dogged determination about them, as if by naming certain things he will keep them secure in his life. "I have lived with integrity ... your love is before my eyes ... I have walked faithfully with you."

Immediately his thoughts are invaded by "the worthless ... the deceitful ... the evildoers." Does he fear that he must take these people into consideration if he is to survive in their kind of world? But he forces these troubling images from his mind, and returns to "the house in which you [Lord] dwell." He seems to run to the temple for sanctuary.

Once more dark images pursue him. He fears being swept away with "sinners ... those who thirst for blood ... Whose hands are full of evil plots ... full of bribes." In desperation he again cries out the determined words he voiced at the beginning of the psalm: "I will live with integrity."

But he realizes that this goal is tremendously difficult in the world where he must function. "Redeem me, O Lord, and have pity on me," he cries. And again comes a sense of calm, a feeling that there are resources available to him. "In the full assembly I will bless the Lord." In a heaving world he has found that his "foot stands on level ground."

When our world presents us with tumultuous cliffs and abysses, may each one of us find such level ground.

∾

Our spiritual life grows through learning to live in the physical world. Try applying your spiritual values to your worldly affairs, and bringing your worldly concerns into your spiritual practice. Ask God to help you reconcile the apparent contradictions.

psalm 27

What if I had not believed
that I should see the goodness of the Lord ...
wait patiently for the Lord.

In her recent book *A History of God*, Karen Armstrong ends a chapter with the following story.

> One day in Auschwitz, a group of Jews put God on trial. They charged [God] with cruelty and betrayal. Like Job, they found no consolation in the usual answers to the problem of evil and suffering in the midst of this current obscenity. They could find no excuse for God, no extenuating circumstances, so they find [God] guilty and, presumably, worthy of death. The Rabbi pronounced the verdict. Then he looked up and said that the trial was over: it was time for the evening prayer.

"Though war should rise up against me, yet will I put my trust in him." So says the psalmist, and he continues to say this in different ways throughout the whole song. He has enemies, and they have attacked. Yet "they stumbled and fell." Even if "an army should encamp against me ... though war should rise ... I will put my trust in him."

This psalm conveys exactly the same impression we gained from the story of the Jews in Auschwitz. We are witnessing something awe-inspiring—an utter and unwavering trust in God.

We are not hearing mere fervent pieties. It is clear that this trust has been won the hard way. "Evildoers came upon me to eat up my flesh." He is extremely well aware of "the day of trouble." Obviously there are "adversaries" and "enemies." There are also those who wound with their tongues. "False witnesses have risen up against me ... also those who speak malice." Yet through all this the trust of the psalmist does not waver.

Is such trust possible? Or is this psalm a lyrical expression of an ideal that remains impossible for all but the greatest souls? There are moments when the vulnerability of the singer sounds. "Hide not your face from me ... cast me not away." We can identify with such feelings and, therefore, with the singer.

The psalmist is admitting that his song is not a boast about possessing impregnable trust. Instead, he prays to be given a measure of trust. Let this prayer also be ours.

≈

Consider adopting a consistent pattern of personal conversation with God. Chat with God many times every day—giving thanks, asking for help, sharing your thoughts. Ask God to strengthen your resolve to build a trusting relationship with God.

Psalm 28

O Lord, I call to you;
my rock, do not be deaf to my cry …
Save your people and bless your inheritance.

Near the end of his life, in one of his letters to Maria von We-demeyer, his fiancée, Dietrich Bonhoeffer wrote that it seemed impossible to find any interior solid ground to stand on in the heaving world of Europe in 1944.

Those of us who live in the world of this later decade can echo that feeling. In the flux of things we seek whatever will stay fixed, even for a short while. In the river of events we seek a rock. "O Lord, I call to you, my rock; do not be deaf to my cry." So pleads the voice of the psalmist.

When you stand in front of one of the gigantic stones that form the base of the Wailing Wall in Jerusalem, it becomes clear why you might begin to think of God as a rock. The image is used frequently in the psalms and all through the Bible. In the wisdom of scripture the rock is never presented as just a mass of stone.

Since the rock is one of countless images for God, there is no danger of God being limited to such an image. Also, this rock pours out a flood of water. In other words, the God who is compared to rock is not only a source of strength, but of refreshment and energy. Because of this rock, "my heart dances for joy."

As the psalmist faces the rock in prayer, he begins to think how unlike God he is. He bluntly states his total dependence on God. "If you do not hear me, I become like those who go down to the Pit." The psalmist's humanity is so weak that it can easily be seduced—very much different from rock. "Do not snatch me away with the wicked." Perhaps the psalmist suspects how likely he might be to suffer the same fate!

Now, as is so often heard in the psalms, the poet moves away from his individual concerns. He has said, "Blessed is the Lord! for he has heard the voice of my prayer." The odds are that most modern prayers or devotional poems would end here. What could be more important than my concerns and my relationship with God?

But the psalm insistently reminds us that we are more than mere individuals. We are members of a body, in our case, the Body of Christ, the People of God. "The Lord is the strength of his people … Save your people and bless your inheritance; shepherd them … carry them."

When we feel vulnerable and defenceless against the forces that would injure us and our world, we need to think and pray more frequently in these terms.

✎

Often we choose to face difficult times alone. We may hesitate to bother others or divulge our problems. Consider how much you depend on others for the necessities and luxuries of life. Pray that you may open yourself to help from God through others.

Psalm 29

The Lord shall give strength to his people;
the Lord shall give his people the blessing of peace.

After the Falklands War, the English prime minister requested a service of worship to give thanks for the victory. In his homily the then Archbishop of Canterbury did not so much celebrate a victory as ask forgiveness for the agony of war. In doing so he provoked much anger.

However, if a victory psalm had been chosen for that service, it could have been this one. "Ascribe to the Lord glory and strength … The voice of the Lord is a powerful voice … the Lord sits enthroned as king for evermore."

This song celebrates the fact that the God of the singers is not only more powerful than the gods of other nations, but is the ruler of all creation. "The Lord is upon the mighty waters … breaks the cedars of Lebanon … makes Lebanon skip … splits the flames of fire … shakes the wilderness … strips the forests bare." Meanwhile, "in the temple of the Lord all are crying, 'Glory!' " while claiming to be "his people."

When we sing this psalm in our own time, we have difficulty assenting to these meanings. We live in a different age and share a different world. We are no longer prepared to say, "Ascribe to the Lord, you gods," as we consider the other great faith traditions of the planet. Ironically, we can concur with the images describing the relationship of God to the natural environment, acknowledging readily that we must bow before a power above our own in these matters.

But the image of the temple where "all are crying, 'Glory!' " is not possible for us in an increasingly secular and fragmented society. This reality makes it increasingly difficult for us to think of ourselves as one people, let alone the people of one God. We may claim hopefully to be one people among many, but this is not the same as the psalmist's idea of one people.

For us, the psalm can be a song giving glory to God. We do not see this deity as the adversary of other visions of God, but as the ultimate reality beyond all such visions. We acknowledge the rule of God over creation, of which we are a part, and for which we have been given responsibility. We worship this God, knowing that others worship in other ways.

Our prayer is that this planet may become the temple of God in which humanity cries "Glory," and that this same humanity may grow to see itself as a single people under God, not merely seeking, but finding, "the blessing of peace."

❧

Consider that all nature, including the earth, is the temple of God, and that all living things, including yourself, are temples of God. Pray that all people may grow to perceive the divine unity in all things, and learn to reverence creation and each other.

Psalm 30

You have turned my wailing into dancing;
you have put off my sack-cloth and clothed me with joy.

There are times when we experience mortal fear, when all we ask is to survive a serious threat. We are not concerned about our pride or dignity. We ask, pray, bargain, and plead. Whether or not we are the kind of person who readily uses religious language, we are in fact pleading with God, if for no other reason than that we are in the realm where life and death meet.

Such things are the matter of this psalm. "O Lord my God, I cried out to you ... I was going down to the grave." This is the language of doctors' offices and hospital corridors, of solitary walks with our own lonely terrible fears.

At such times we can realize how much we take life for granted, how sweet its seemingly ordinary things can be when we face the possibility of losing them, and how we can come to trust in our own strength and abilities. "While I felt secure, I said, 'I shall never be disturbed. You Lord ... made me as strong as the mountains.' "

But our experience is full of surprises. "Then you hid your face, and I was filled with fear." Suddenly there is shocking change in our lives. A phone rings, a letter is opened, a carefully measured voice gives us a diagnosis, a relationship is hurt by the discovery of betrayal. Light changes to darkness; music falls silent. Our own voice is that of the psalmist. "I go down to the Pit ... have mercy ... Lord, be my helper."

Now comes the voice of other times we have known. "You

have lifted me up … You restored me to health." We recognize the surge of returning life in such moments when a great shadow has been lifted. We want to share the good news. We find ourselves laughing and babbling our relief, as does the psalmist. "My heart sings to you … I will give you thanks!"

Now that the terror is lifted, we forget the hours of fear and worry that became weeks and even months. The threat, the feeling of life betraying us, the thought of God being angry at us for some reason—all seem now to be "but the twinkling of an eye." The pleading and the promises have become memories. If we dared to be completely truthful, perhaps they are even a little embarrassing.

But whatever our subsequent days may be after such an experience, we have had a clear glass held before us. We have seen deeply into our humanity, and learned its need for grace beyond itself.

~

Consider some of the important things in life that you tend to take for granted. Thank God for these things. Consider people, both near to you and far from you, who lack such things. Ask God to give those who "have" compassion for those who "have not."

Psalm 31

Blessed be the Lord!
for he has shown me the wonders of his love
in a besieged city.

Perhaps in one aspect, the Book of Psalms is not unlike an opera. There are long passages of recitative that are neither exciting nor attractive musically. But suddenly, sometimes when one is least expecting it, there comes a beautiful aria that grips the attention and moves the emotions.

There is such a verse in this psalm. The poet is reflecting on a particularly difficult phase of life. There are some hints that age may be more and more on his mind, but let us return to this later. For now, one verse flashes out: "Blessed be the Lord! for he has shown me the wonders of his love in a besieged city."

This verse speaks on many levels. First, in the literal meaning of the word "city." The modern city, where most of us live, is in many senses besieged by problems that sometimes seem beyond solution, certainly beyond easy solution. But there is also the little city, the inner city, the city of the human soul, always in some ways under siege.

The armies of responsibility, tension, stress, and anxiety surround this little city, sometimes playing havoc with it, sometimes collapsing its walls and destroying its streets. Yet even while we are under such siege, it is possible to look about us and see some "wonders of [God's] love"—experiences, discoveries, sometimes small achievements, so many supports that have made it possible for our inner city to withstand those things that would lay siege to it.

For each one of us, these wonders will be different. For one, it will be a loving relationship given as a gift far beyond our deserving. For another, it will be the sudden realization of how much a long taken-for-granted friendship means. It can be the immense satisfaction of a job well done. It may be the things of beauty that give us grace—music, art, great writing. It may be the liturgy of the church. All these things can be "the wonders of [God's] love" in our sometimes besieged inner city.

The psalmist tells us of the things that besiege him. There is some great sorrow. He has a sense of life slipping away, of control being lost. "My strength fails me … I am useless as a broken pot." Yet always for the psalmist there is the Lord who gives grace, and a new grasp on life. "Be strong and let your heart take courage, all you who wait for the Lord."

May we also turn to the Lord—not only in our adversity but every day—and find abundant grace for our living.

≈

Recall someone struggling with the anxiety of being near the end of life. Recall someone besieged by the tension of serious responsibility. Ask God to be with these people, to strengthen and comfort them, and to be with you, when you face such circumstances.

Psalm 32

I acknowledged my sin to you,
and did not conceal my guilt.

Recently I answered the phone, and a familiar voice cried out, "I've just heard the news. He's not guilty." For some months the case had gone on, dragging through the judicial system. It had hung over many lives, not just the accused.

There were ghastly days when it seemed as if the arguments for the defence would fail. Now there was immense relief and joy. I could hear it in every tremor of the voice on the phone. Two words had changed everything: "not guilty." Life and freedom had been given back for the living.

"Happy are they whose transgressions are forgiven, and whose sin is put away!" Here is the theme of this psalm. Someone has emerged from bearing a heavy load of guilt, and they are now revelling in their newfound freedom. "Happy are they to whom the Lord imputes no guilt."

There are many kinds of guilt and many sources—as we all know. There is the guilt we heap on ourselves for some word or action. We would give anything to unsay or undo whatever it is. Such guilt can be carried inside us, for a long time and at great cost. It can eat away at us.

"While I held my tongue, my bones withered away ... your hand was heavy upon me day and night; my moisture was dried up as in the heat of summer." Many of us know these symptoms—a kind of aching inside oneself, a sense of things bearing down, a deep listlessness and lack of interest in life. All these feelings can accompany unresolved guilt.

Now comes a moment when the burden cannot be borne any longer and must be shared. We are not told what brings on this moment of decision, but suddenly it is there. "I said, 'I will confess my transgressions to the Lord.'" Notice the instantaneous sense of being forgiven. The psalmist doesn't even pause to give the verse the usual two-line parallel form, so characteristic of the psalms.

Instead, as if the news is too good to be true, he exclaims, "You [Lord] forgave me the guilt of my sin." Immediately he wants to share his experience with anyone who will listen. "All the faithful will make their prayers to you in time of trouble ... mercy embraces those who trust in the Lord ... shout for joy, all who are true of heart."

As we listen, we realize that we have just heard across the centuries a testimony to the immensely healing power of confession—renewing us, re-energizing us, giving back our life.

≈

Guilty memories can weigh us down, and sap our energy and joy. Opening your soul can help to heal the wound. Consider sharing these memories with God, and with a trusted friend or counsellor. Ask God to support you, and give you grace and healing.

Psalm 33

There is no king that can be saved by a mighty army;
a strong man is not delivered by his great strength.

Dag Hammarskjöld, who headed the United Nations in the early days of the Cold War, successfully hid from the world that, among many other things, he was a deeply spiritual man. After his death the world learned of this spirituality in his writings, especially in a book called *Markings*.

Among its many cryptic statements is Hammarskjöld's reference to his spiritual conversion. He writes, "At some moment I did answer Yes to Someone—or Something—and from that hour I was certain that existence is meaningful and that, therefore, my life, in self-surrender, had a goal." In such simple language Hammarskjöld revealed the source of his strength and his great political influence.

In this psalm the writer reflects about the nature of power, and immediately places its source in God. The very first words do this: "Rejoice in the Lord." There follows a description of the character of God. "The word of the Lord is right ... [God] loves righteousness and justice ... [and] loving-kindness."

For the writer, God is involved in the events of history. "The Lord brings the will of the nations to naught." God alone is the source of any power worth having. "Happy is the nation whose God is the Lord!"

The psalmist is wise enough to realize that the obvious sources of power can sometimes prove deceiving. "There is no king that can be saved by a mighty army; a strong man is not delivered by his great strength." In these two vivid images he tells us that, if we do not possess resources beyond ourselves, our personal power can disintegrate, despite all our posturing and carefully erected defences. If we are wise, we will see that "our soul waits for the Lord."

The psalm writer is under no illusions about the source of personal strength. Not for a moment is he saying that God is a convenience for us to depend on, a substitute for our resolve and effort. Instead "the Lord … is our help and our shield … in his holy name we put our trust."

Being mindful and assured of the divine source of all our power, we can decide and act with confidence.

✎

When there is something you want to achieve, spend time to clarify your purpose, plan the operation, gather the information, and assemble the materials. During all stages of the process, continually consult with God, and seek guidance from God.

Psalm 34

Taste and see that the Lord is good;
happy are they who trust in him!

Often as I read a psalm, a single verse, sometimes a single phrase, will leap off the page and speak.

"Look upon [the Lord] and be radiant," says the psalmist. Immediately I think of how fascinated today's culture is with looking not at the Lord, but at the self. So much in our society seems to say, "Look upon yourself, study yourself, examine yourself, travel down deep inside yourself, and eventually you will be radiant!" In a time of many harmful directives, some of them generated by great industries, this can be one of the most misleading.

Listening again to the psalmist we hear, "Proclaim with me the greatness of the Lord." Again we find an apparent head-on contradiction with something promulgated repeatedly in our culture. Voices, images, articles, gurus say to us, "Realize your potential! Discover your own greatness! Become who you are!" On and on go the seductive mantras.

But both of these exhortations—one from the psalm and the other from our culture—carry within them a deep truth. It is indeed vital to study oneself, to examine oneself, and to realize one's potential. But this potential is other than superficial voices imagine!

In Genesis 1:27 we learn that we are made "in the image of God," and in Galatians 2:20 Paul asserts, "It is no longer I who live, but it is Christ who lives in me." This is the source of our true potential. The inner quest can be harmful when it remains superficial, stopping at the narrow ego—the self we show to the world—instead of probing through the ego to the wide inner reality, to seek our Lord at the centre of our being.

For the psalmist, the quest never ends at the superficial level. It reaches through the ego and delves toward that which is infinitely deeper and greater. The quest of self-discovery leads toward the discovery God. "I will bless the Lord at all times … I will glory in the Lord."

The psalmist is saying to us that our journey into the self must not be satisfied with false truths but only with the ultimate truth. When he says to us, "The Lord … delivered me … saved me," he is telling us that "deliverance," "salvation," and "happiness" lie with God alone.

We may wish to use other words for these things. We may speak of the ultimate meaning, or the reason for living with a measure of joy and hope in the world. The psalmist places the source of this ultimate meaning in God. "Taste and see that the Lord is good," he says to us. "Happy are they who trust in him!"

❧

When you can be quiet and alone, delve deeply into yourself. Identify some personal attributes that you feel may originate with God, and some that you feel may not. Ask God for courage to face the false truths, and for strength to realize your ultimate truth.

Psalm 35

Awake, arise to my cause!
to my defence, my God and my Lord!

When St. Paul was writing his letter to the Christian community in Rome, he became deeply personal. He spoke of a war going on inside him, as if mysterious powers were battling for his allegiance. There was something inside him that prevented him from doing the good he wished to do, and sometimes even made him do the evil he did not want to do!

This may suggest a helpful way for us to approach psalms such as this. From beginning to end it is populated by the psalmist's enemies. The opening verses are desperate and gasping shouts for help. "Fight those who fight me, O Lord … Draw the sword … against those who pursue me."

From this plea for help the psalmist moves to a long malediction of his enemies. "Let [them] be shamed … Let them be like chaff … Let ruin come upon them … let them fall into the pit they dug."

There follows a recitation of the things he has suffered. "Malicious witnesses … gathered against me … tore me to pieces and would not stop … rejoice at my ruin." In his trouble the psalmist repeatedly calls upon God. "O Lord, how long will you look on? … Give me justice, O Lord my God."

To say that we might read all this as if the enemies are inside rather than outside is not to deny that we do sometimes face external enemies. We can encounter them frequently in our professional lives. There are people who have been determined in various ways to discredit or destroy us, and we have had to take steps to protect ourselves.

Sometimes, when all other measures have failed, we have had to assert ourselves to survive. Certain verses of this psalm express this vividly. "They pay me evil in exchange for good ... I prayed with my whole heart, as one would for a friend ... But when I stumbled, they were glad ... and mocked me."

The truth is that enemies and friends exist both within and about us. Our inner enemies are our various weaknesses; our inner friends are the gifts and strengths we own—in either case, we are aware of some and blind to others. We are usually aware of our outer enemies and friends, but not always.

The psalmist speaks of his friends. "Let those who favour my cause sing out." Our own prayer to God might be that we become as aware of our friends—both inner and outer—as we are of our enemies. Above all, our prayer can be that we remain alert to the presence of God as friend in the face of our enemies.

≈

When you discover an unacceptable characteristic in another person, consider looking for this same characteristic in yourself. Ask God for courage and grace to discover and face your own short-comings, as well as the shortcomings you discover in others.

Psalm 36

For with you is the well of life,
and in your light we see light.

Rudyard Kipling once described art created on a vast scale as "splashing at a ten-league canvas with brushes of comet's hair." In vivid stories that convey this quality of vastness, the Bible explores the themes of wickedness and the immeasurable love of God.

"There is a voice of rebellion deep in the heart of the wicked." In the Bible the essence of all wickedness is rebellion against the rule of God. This is true in Eden, where human willfulness is pitted against the will and plan of God. It is also true in the glimpse of cosmic war given to us in the letter of Jude, where the great archangel Lucifer defies God, leads a rebellion, and is thrown from heaven.

These events are acted out on a great timeless stage outside of history. But the Bible points out that the same things also hold true in our own seemingly ordinary lives. The psalmist says of the wicked, "There is no fear of God before his eyes ... he has left off acting wisely."

Wickedness originates at the moment when a human being decides that he or she is the centre of things, that his or her intentions and motives are ultimate, and then begins to act accordingly. "[The wicked] flatters himself in his own eyes ... has set himself in no good way."

Because the psalmist is aware that he himself is an "inner country," where forces battle to possess his allegiance, he asks for help from God. He knows that those who choose evil think about it a great deal. "He thinks up wickedness upon his bed."

The psalmist knows that our thoughts shape us. The more we become fascinated by a certain way of looking at the world, the more this mental attitude determines our actions. So the psalmist deliberately chooses to concentrate his thoughts on the nature of God, the source of goodness. "Your love, O Lord, reaches to the heavens … Your righteousness is like the strong mountains … How priceless is your love!"

The psalmist is hoping that the love and righteousness of God will become the driving forces within him. In a beautiful image he finds himself drinking deeply of God: "with you is the well of life." And in the finest line of the psalm he says of God: "in your light we see light."

It is by looking beyond our very undependable self to the utterly dependable reality of God that we find grace for our needs, light for our choices, and direction for our way forward.

❧

Are there moments when you know what is right to think or do, but you decide to proceed against your conscience? Be honest but gentle with yourself. Ask God to strengthen the image of God within you, and to guide you in the better way.

Psalm 37

Be still before the Lord and wait patiently for him.
Do not fret yourself over the one who prospers,
the one who succeeds in evil schemes.

One very annoying thing for decent people is that, at least in the short term, being unscrupulous seems to pay handsomely. Some other questionable activities also reap hefty rewards, for a while—playing the power game, not caring for people who get in the way, fiddling certain key accounts. Such codes of conduct often produce many pleasant things we might all like to have.

The prospering of the unscrupulous is doubly annoying because, while we do not admire their wrongdoing, we cannot help envying their gains. It is important for us to admit this. The psalmist captures this insight perfectly, not once but again and again. "Do not fret," we are advised no less than three times, precisely because we do indeed fret a great deal about the injustices of life.

And we get angry. But if we are prepared to be honest with ourselves, we know that our anger arises not purely because of the questionable methods of some people so much as their exasperating successes and our consequent envy, which we have already acknowledged. "Refrain from anger," says the psalmist, "leave rage alone." This is excellent advice. There is perhaps nothing more useless than the anger born of envy.

Again, if we are honest, the alternative suggested by the psalmist does not really excite us. Essentially, he is saying, "What little the righteous have is better than the wealth of the wicked." In our cynical moments we may find this dictum less than persuasive.

However, in the long haul of life, which is exactly what the psalmist is getting at, we will come to know and savour the depth of his words. Those who "wait upon the Lord [will] possess the land." This may not be literally true. But it is true with respect to our inner land, the country of our own soul and integrity.

One salutary consequence of being Christian is our belief that eventually we will need not only to make peace with the way we have lived, but also to answer to one greater than ourselves.

∾

Consider someone who uses hurtful methods to succeed. Ask yourself what deep needs drive this person. Ask God to help them heal. Ask God to save you from anger and envy, and to help you realize the gifts and riches in your own life.

Psalm 38

In you, O Lord, have I fixed my hope;
you will answer me, O Lord my God.

Every so often, in reading the psalms I am struck by the differ-
ence between the mind of the psalmist and the minds of most
people today.

God is the source of all experience for the psalmist—not merely
the source of grace, to be turned to when life is grim, but also the
source of present misery. The psalmist's first words name this source
simply and clearly. "O Lord, do not rebuke me in your anger; do
not punish me in your wrath."

In recent years Western thinking has come round to the view
that what goes on in our mind and heart is inescapably reflected
in our body. In this respect our views are converging with those of
the psalmist. He sees no separation between the physical and the
moral. "There is no soundness in my body, because of my sin." And
again, "My wounds stink and fester by reason of my foolishness."

Until recently in Western culture these statements would
have been dismissed as irrational, even superstitious, but much is
happening to change this attitude. We are increasingly learning
to appreciate the mysterious ways in which human experience is
a seamless unity, and cannot be divided into arbitrary unrelated
compartments. This sounds so clearly in the psalms.

"My loins are filled with searing pain." Nothing could be more
physical. "I go about in mourning all the day long." We hear the
distinct ring of depression. "My friends and companions draw

back from my affliction." These words express growing isolation. "Those who strive to hurt me speak of my ruin." Now there is self-pitying fear.

We cannot help wondering how much of his own character and experience the psalmist is projecting on to others. Who exactly is withdrawing from social contact? To what extent is depression passing into alienation?

At this point we realize a wonderful thing. The questions we have just asked are very much of our own time. They are all asked in the domain of the narrow ego self, with all its limitations. But precisely because the psalmist regards God as the ultimate reality, he has a resource beyond himself to turn to.

The unwillingness to accept an ultimate power beyond ourselves has been devastating for millions of people in recent decades. Human ingenuity and strength alone are woefully inadequate to the task of negotiating all the curves that life can pitch at us.

But recent signs of a return to the acceptance of an ultimate power are deeply encouraging. "In you, O Lord, have I fixed my hope; you will answer me, O Lord my God."

⁓

Persistent negative feelings and thoughts can sometimes trouble us. Eventually they may affect our physical lives. Consider inviting God to protect and guide you. Ask God to give you strength and insight, and to help you reach the positive through the negative.

Psalm 39

Turn your gaze from me, that I may be glad again,
before I go my way and am no more.

As we read the opening verses, we are made aware of many moments in our own experience. "I said, 'I will keep watch upon my ways, so that I do not offend' … So I held my tongue … but my pain became unbearable."

We all know this experience well. We make resolutions to keep ourselves under control, to hide our anger or indignation or sense of being wronged. But we so often fail. Like the psalmist, "While I pondered, the fire burst into flame; I spoke out."

We can never know the exact situation that triggers thoughts such as these, but what comes next suggests that the psalmist is wrestling with a sense of futility. "My lifetime is as nothing in your sight … but a puff of wind." He seems to be tired of trying to deal with others around him who do not always wish him well, tired of trying to change his own personality so that he can handle situations in a better way.

Again, we know the mood well, one in which we sometimes throw up our hands and say, "What's the use!" The psalmist too cries, "Do not make me the taunt of the fool … I am worn down by the blows of your hand."

Again the psalmist has no compunction in saying that God is the source of his trouble. "I fell silent and did not open my mouth, for surely it was you that did it." But with this knowledge—and this is so easy for us to forget—there comes the conviction that there is some meaning to what is happening in his life. Because he can say, "Surely it was you that did it," he can also say, "Hear my prayer, O Lord, and give ear to my cry."

The very last verse contains an intriguing wrinkle that we can easily miss. The psalmist asks God, "Turn your gaze from me, that I may be glad again." There exists a great deal of sentimental prayer asking God to be aware of us forever. But are there not some things about us that we would prefer God did not know? Would we not prefer to keep these things hidden even from ourselves?

The psalmist is more realistic. When the divine eyes are upon us, is it not possible that God will be aware of something particularly unattractive in our soul? If we really want the gaze of God upon us, we will need to face the fact that some painful reconstruction may be needed for what God sees!

The prayer sounds strange to our ears, but it may sometimes be a wise and even necessary one. "Turn your gaze from me, that I may be glad again."

Are there some occasions in your life that you would rather not remember, that you would rather God certainly did not see? Ask God to let you visit these memories with gentleness, and help you find loving acceptance and healing grace for them.

Psalm 40

In the roll of the book it is written concerning me:
"I love to do your will, O my God."

There are people who seem to possess an unquenchable joy. To be in their company is a constant pleasure and inspiration. Some of their joy is transmitted to us. We can feel it, and we often wish we could capture it, as they have.

But what is most remarkable about these people is that they often endure circumstances that are anything but cause for joy. They may have experienced great loss, or they may be in constant pain, yet their suffering does not seem to diminish their extraordinary capacity for joy.

We hear something of this capacity in these verses. "I waited patiently upon the Lord," says the psalmist. "He lifted me out of the desolate pit … he set my feet upon a high cliff … He put a new song in my mouth … Happy are they who trust in the Lord!" But later in the song, as we listen again, we hear a different story. "Innumerable troubles have crowded upon me … [There are] those who say 'Aha!' and gloat over me … I am poor and afflicted."

It would seem that to be lifted out of the "desolate pit," to be set upon a "high cliff," and to have a "new song" does not mean being relieved of all our troubles. It does mean, however, that God is able to "put a new song in my mouth," even as we continue to wrestle with our troubles. The difficulties are still real and present. What has changed is our response to them.

This change manifests for the psalmist when he decides to take responsibility for his own life. In his culture it was customary to petition God with sacrifices—a kind of bargaining. The psalmist has decided that this is no longer enough. "Burnt-offering and sin-offering you have not required."

But what is it, then, that God does require? In a breakthrough in the thinking of the poet, which is also a breakthrough in the way Judaism itself conceived of God, the psalmist says, "I said, 'Behold, I come.' " The significance lies in the personal pronoun "I."

Notice how there is a succession of sharply emphasized repetitions of the pronoun. "'I love to do your will, O my God' … I proclaimed righteousness … I have spoken of your faithfulness." The psalmist realizes that what has to be given to God is his very self, so that his self may find, and be filled with, a source of joy and meaning beyond itself.

∽

Consider a current anxiety or affliction—great or small—in your life. Invite God to share the experience with you fully. Allow your whole being to flow into the presence of God, and allow the presence of God to flow into your whole being.

psalm 41

Happy are the who consider the poor and needy!
the Lord will deliver them in the time of trouble.

∂ s I read this psalm, I ask myself how much this reflection of
mine would mean to someone who might happen to stumble on
it twenty-five hundred years in the future. All sorts of assumptions
I make will no longer apply in that far-off time. Understandings
about human nature and experience may be radically different.

Then I realize with wonder how much the psalms speak to my
experience after the same period of time. This is clear proof, if we
need it, of the greatness of these ancient songs.

Consider the unexpected direction in which this psalm takes
our thinking. Its first word is "happy," its first thought for "the
poor and needy." But almost immediately we are made aware of
the presence of enemies. They populate the rest of the psalm in
abundance! They are present as threatening, even terrifying voices,
"saying wicked things about me: 'When will he die?' ... They speak
empty words; their heart collects false rumours ... [they] spread
them ... whisper together ... devise evil ... Even my best friend
[has] turned against me."

Enemies crop up so frequently in the psalms that we need
to decide what their presence means for us. It is true that no one
among us is totally without those who do not like us and do not
particularly wish us well. It is also true that those who wish us
actual harm and are prepared to act on their wish are usually few.

And at least some of the enemies that appear in the psalms

must be numbered among the adversaries to which we give birth inside ourselves. Everyone knows the voice that begins to speak to us when we are worried about some physical ailment or recurring pain or inconclusive medical test. "A deadly thing … has fastened on [me]," says this voice.

And while this affliction dwells within us, it is no less an enemy. Such enemies can severely sap our strength. They can cast dark shadows over our best efforts to live fully in spite of them. They can "devise evil against me."

Surrounded by all this talk of enemies, it is easy for us to forget the opening verses of this psalm. But when we do look back, we find these verses saying an extraordinarily beautiful thing. The psalmist gives us an antidote to being oppressed by life. He tells us that to "consider the poor and needy" is truly healing.

A readiness to give sweetens life against those many acids that can make life bitter and even corrode it. We shall let the psalmist state this glorious truth in his own words. "The Lord preserves" those who consider the needy, "and keeps them alive."

✍

Consider some present trouble or affliction that is weighing heavily in your life. Now give thought to some person or group of people less fortunate than yourself. Offer a prayer that God may comfort and assist them in their need, and you in your need.

Psalm 42

Why are you so full of heaviness, O my soul?
and why are you so disquieted within me?

On any journey we may come to some turn in the road, some clearing in the trees, some cove or headland where the heart lifts and the hand instinctively points to share the discovery with others. This psalm affords such an experience. To say this is not to dismiss other landscapes on the journey, but merely to say that here is a place of special beauty.

"As the deer longs for the water-brooks, so longs my soul for you, O God." Not only is this image one of infinite beauty and gracefulness; even the words that give us the image are full of soft languorous consonants linked by long sonorous vowels. Also, this psalm serves as a kind of oasis where we meet all those across the centuries who have found it to be a sweet well of grace. The voices of so many have said with the psalmist, "My soul is athirst for God, athirst for the living God."

This psalm brings us to a part of the spiritual journey that is not easily travelled. If we are prepared to identify with the experience of the psalmist, then we have a sense of being probed deeply. "Where now is your God?" says the voice to him and, at times, to us. How real is my faith? What do I really believe? Would my faith stand testing? Am I merely pretending, using up the capital of an earlier faith, carrying out long-learned rituals? These questions can be profoundly disturbing. "I pour out my soul when I think on these things."

We find ourselves wandering through the badlands of the soul. A voice asks again and again, "Why are you so full of heaviness, O my soul? and why are you so disquieted within me?" The question can be deeply frustrating because there may be no discernible reason for this great shadow looming over our spirit.

Things that have normally served to refresh us no longer do so. "I went with the multitude and led them into the house of God, With the voice of praise and thanksgiving." The psalmist seems to imply that even the beauty of liturgy and architecture has grown dull and empty, having lost the capacity to inspire.

Once again we arrive at the place where the psalmist brings us so often. We encounter the terrible beauty and ultimacy of God. Heaviness and disquiet there may be, but greater than this is trust and thanksgiving. "I will yet give thanks to him, who is the help of my countenance, and my God.

≈

Have there been times in your life when you longed for the love and power and beauty of God? Have there been times in your life when you sensed the presence of God around and within you? Be vigilant for such moments. Thank God for such moments.

Psalm 43

Put your trust in God ...
who is the help of my countenance, and my God.

If we need any proof that the poetry of the psalms knows human
nature intimately, we get such proof in the question asked by the
psalmist again and again. "Why are you so full of heaviness, O
my soul? and why are you so disquieted within me?" Every word
is familiar to us because each one of us has asked ourselves this
question.

This is not the only psalm in which we hear such a question,
perhaps because the question comes not only at times of great crisis
in our spiritual journey. Strangely, various other kinds of crisis are
often more easily dealt with than the recurring and implacable
sieges to our inner citadel. But for good or ill, with one result or
another, crises come. We do our wrestling and find ourselves victor
or vanquished.

But those times when we feel an absence of God, the loss of
meaning and joy in life, come upon us without warning. The psalm-
ist's self-questioning has a puzzled and almost aggrieved tone: "you
are the God of my strength." We like to think of favourable times
as the norm for our spirituality. "Why have you put me from you?
and why do I go so heavily while the enemy oppresses me?"

Then in the mind of the psalmist, as we would say today, a
light goes on. "Send out your light and your truth, that they may
lead me." But this is no dazzling light from ourselves, unless we

count as brilliant our realization that we alone are not sufficient for this task.

The soul seems like an army under siege. The moment arrives when resistance can no longer be kept up. And the soul realizes that it is time to turn for help, to say to another and a greater power, "Defend my cause."

Sigmund Freud held that humanity has become dependent on religion. It is always puzzling how effectively Freud's charge of dependency has stuck to religious faith. After all, there is no area of our lives where we are not in some sense dependent. Is it not true that this dependency on every side of us in daily life is merely the sign of the dependency of all creation on the God who created it? "Put your trust in God ... who is the help of my countenance, and my God."

We bow our heads in unashamed dependence, and we go "to the altar of God, to the God of [our] joy and gladness."

❧

How often in life have you felt that you must face and resolve your problems on your own? Ask God to help you realize your dependency on other people and on the grace of God. Supportive relationships give strength. Take courage and ask for help.

Psalm 44

You have made us a byword among the nations …
My humiliation is daily before me.

Every now and again, as we read the psalms we get a mental jolt. Some word, some image, some thought, some way of expressing a thought, serves to remind us that we and the psalmist think differently. Clearly, we do inhabit different worlds. It is important to notice when we feel these jolts. They can prompt us to examine much that we take for granted about the way things should be.

In the opening verses the psalmist is recalling the history of his people. "Our forefathers have told us, the deeds you did in their days … you … made your people flourish … you favoured them." Suddenly we hear a very personal statement. "You are my King and my God." But then we learn that "they did not take the land … nor did their arm win the victory for them." This is followed by another personal claim. "I do not rely on my bow."

In the mind of the psalmist the individual and his society are so closely linked that what is true of one is also true of the other. Later on this is even more marked. "You have made us the scorn of our neighbours … a byword among the nations," followed by, "My humiliation is daily before me."

Perhaps we can let the verses of this psalm jolt us into looking at our own situation today. In our culture the prosperity of the individual is far more important than the welfare of the society. As the claims of the individual on the society grow, the claims of the society on the individual diminish, or at least are questioned and resented.

As the psalmist searches for the reasons why his people seem to be weaker, so do many today search for an explanation why our society has arrived at its present state. From his long-ago context the psalmist poses an essential question: "If we have forgotten the name of our God, or stretched out our hands to some strange god, Will not God find it out?" In what terms today can we begin to frame such a question, and how can we begin to find an answer to it?

"[God] knows the secrets of the heart," says the psalmist, and we can assume that he means not only an individual heart, but the heart of a society.

*

Consider some ways in which the society around you is suffering. How does this suffering impinge on your own life? Ask God to comfort the unfortunate and suffering, and to inspire the fortunate and powerful to alleviate the suffering in society.

Psalm 45

Your throne, O God, endures for ever and ever,
a sceptre of righteousness is the sceptre of your kingdom.

About two and a half millennia ago, a king is crowned. A poem is composed for the occasion. The verses find their way into the treasury of the nation's poetry, and eventually end up in the canon of its sacred books, which centuries later become the sacred books of a worldwide religion. And so we find ourselves reading this poem in Christian public worship today.

Like many verses in the Bible, this poem is interpreted allegorically today. After all, the actual king holds no significance for us. Yet the more we read these verses, the more they tell us about the way that kingship and leadership and public responsibility were seen in Israel long ago.

In this poem we hear certain timeless assumptions that we forget at our peril. "Grace flows from your lips," sings the psalmist for the king. But why? "Because God has blessed you for ever." This is important for us to hear. "Ride out and conquer," sings the poet. But to what purpose? "In the cause of truth and for the sake of justice." The poet tells the king about a throne that "endures for ever and ever," but only if it is recognized as God's throne, and only if the king holds "a sceptre of righteousness."

Every aspect of kingship identified in this psalm is examined for the source of its integrity. Every aspect of the ruler's authority is seen to flow from beyond the ruler himself. Authority derives from God alone. The anointing of the ruler is the act of God giving grace, which the ruler himself does not possess. Centuries have passed, yet these timeless assumptions have formed the great democratic societies of our time.

The woman to be queen is also addressed with the assumptions of the time. She is reminded that she will wield her own kind of power. "The rich among the people seek your favour." She and the king together, if they are so blessed, will become the bearers of the future, "from one generation to another."

To say that these assumptions about authority in society have formed the traditions of democratic societies down through history, including our own, is not to claim that these societies are perfect. We know there is much in our world that corrodes and diminishes these assumptions. But they have not yet yielded their power to attract and inspire men and women.

Today, as in the past, if a governing system is to be a "throne [that] endures," then its integrity must be apparent. In the words of the psalmist, such an enduring governing system must bear a "sceptre of righteousness." Even today, to sing of these things is to feel one's heart "stirring with a noble song."

❧

What are some of the primary assumptions of a democratic society? To what extent do these assumptions pertain in your society? Pray that the rulers of your society, and all societies, may discover the source of their responsibility and authority in God.

Psalm 46

God is our refuge and strength ...
The Lord of hosts is with us.

Once again we encounter a psalm that becomes a well, an oasis, where we meet those who have arrived here before us in time. Two that come to mind immediately are Martin Luther, who gave us the hymn "Ein Feste Burg" from this psalm, and Isaac Watts, who visited this sweet well two centuries later and drew from its waters the lines we know as "O God, our help in ages past, our hope for years to come."

This psalm possesses greatness because it reaches for a vision of the majesty of God. We must say "reaches," since the ultimate majesty of God is beyond human comprehension, and certainly beyond language.

As the great sculptors of classical Greece reached to capture the human form, as Picasso reached to express in his canvas *Guernica* the terrible essence of war and suffering, so the psalmist pursues the majesty of God, using the most awe-inspiring natural phenomena as a backdrop to his song. "Though the earth be moved ... though the mountains be toppled into the depths of the sea; Though its waters rage and foam ... though the mountains tremble ... the Lord of hosts is with us."

A claim made in the opening words of this psalm may be the most audacious ever made by human thought. "God is our refuge and strength ... The Lord of hosts is with us." This claim asserts that the Creator of the universe is in some way concerned about our humanity.

The claim goes further. It asks us to believe that our humanity is mysteriously instrumental in the unimaginably vast cosmic plan of this Creator. No wonder many find this impossible to believe. And millions of people who try to believe it have never remotely glimpsed the immensity of what they are saying.

Within the psalm there is the flash of a vision that has haunted humanity ever since we began to form communities and societies. "The city of God, the holy habitation of the Most High. God is in the midst of her." This vision of God at the heart of human society has called and inspired countless men and women down through history.

This vision has energized people, often at great personal cost, to work and to struggle, sometimes even to fight, for such things as integrity, justice, reconciliation, freedom, peace. Such is the power of this psalm.

❧

Can you think of certain times in history when it is clear that God was guiding humanity? Can you think of times in your life when God has guided you? Pray that you may always be mindful of God and be open to the guidance of God.

Psalm 47

Clap your hands, all you peoples;
shout to God with a cry of joy.

We are obviously in a crowd, and we are caught up in a rhythm of joyous praise. Since this has happened to all of us at one time or another, we can easily enter into this psalm. We can imagine bodies swaying as the crowd moves. Faces are upturned, most are smiling, some arms are raised, some hands are clapping, and—unless human nature has changed greatly over the centuries—a few people are thinking that sometimes enthusiasm can get a little out of hand!

This is a good psalm to remind us of the grace and gifts we receive in public worship. "Clap your hands, all you peoples; shout to God with a cry of joy."

One important gift is the assurance of solidarity with other people who hold certain things in common with us. A personal faith needs this assurance. Without times of communal gathering, a personal faith is vulnerable to emotional forces that sweep over the human spirit. Also, there is a need to counteract the temptation to understand Christian faith as a completely individual journey.

Notice that God is mentioned in every single verse of this psalm. Notice too how the nature of God is constantly understood in terms of activity. God "subdues the peoples ... chooses our inheritance ... has gone up with a shout ... reigns over the nations." This strongly implies that the people who worship such a God express their faith in action.

The implication of an active faith does not in the least invalidate introspection, but merely demands that it issue in action. This demand is particularly necessary in our time, when there is a tendency to regard Christian faith as merely the source of inner meaning and inner peace.

Everything said about God in these verses highlights the transcendence of God. "God is king of all the earth … is highly exalted." The psalms do not neglect to speak of God as present in the human heart and spirit, but here the emphasis points outward.

Our present time needs the vision of God as transcendent. Our culture, where it does seek God, is given to the inner search. As soon as our whole being is oriented toward the ultimate reality beyond ourselves, then we are freed from being captive to our own egocentric concerns. Our narrow everyday world is vastly expanded and uplifted by the glory of God, "highly exalted."

&

Christianity regards God as both immanent (living in us and all created things) and transcendent (living beyond us and all created things). Imagine some implications of God's immanence, and of God's transcendence. Seek to know God more and more.

Psalm 48

Make the circuit of Zion ...
count the number of her towers ...
that you may tell those who come after.

On reading this psalm I want to make a cultural link that may seem incongruous and unworthy of its sacred theme. We hear the psalmist indulging in a vivid and emotional celebration of a place—the city of Jerusalem centred around the Hill of Zion. And I am reminded of contemporary songs about modern cities—perhaps, more than any other, the voice of Tony Bennett plaintively singing, "I left my heart in San Francisco."

In this psalm also we hear someone pour out their heart, as they look on a city they love and treasure. "Beautiful and lofty, the joy of all the earth, is the hill of Zion, the very centre of the world and the city of the great king." To this day, as one stands on the western slopes of the Mount of Olives, looking toward Mount Zion, one can capture some of the sense of pride we hear in these lines.

There still remains a mysterious quality to this city, in spite of all the tides of cruelty and war and hatred that have swept across it. The psalmist alludes to this. "The kings of the earth assembled and marched forward together." So they did, century after century, in successive invasions.

The psalmist's claim that "they retreated and fled in terror" may not be literally true. It was certainly not true for the Tenth Legion of the Roman army in AD 70. Yet, long after the empire of the Romans has become a memory, Jerusalem stands, even as it wrestles with its contemporary agonies.

As one listens to the psalmist saying, "The city of our God … God is in her citadels … God has established her for ever," we find ourselves asking what this language means. Is there any sense in which we are prepared to believe that God is in the structures and institutions of our own country? We have almost lost the capacity to think in these terms, yet such a loss may have a high price. To think about our society as the dwelling place of God need not be an arrogant and self-aggrandizing claim. But we are not at all denying the presence of God to other societies and cultures.

The psalmist himself suggests a reason why a sense of the presence of God is important. "God is in her citadels," he writes, "[God] is known to be her sure refuge." What is being suggested to us is this—a society that owns the presence of God in its life is a society that can draw on a source of strength other than its own.

⟿

Consider a town or city you know well. In what places do you sense God's presence? In what places do you not sense God's presence? Pray that the citizens of this town or city may learn to seek, and find, God's presence in these places.

Psalm 49

The ransom of our life is so great,
that we should never have enough to pay it.

To read this psalm is to hear the echo of a well-known voice. One of the most intriguing writers in the whole canon of scripture is the charming teacher who gave us the book Ecclesiastes. The fact that we know nothing about him makes him even more intriguing. For some reason, when I read this psalm, I wonder if I am hearing his voice again, whether or not he is the psalmist in this case.

Quite probably some helpful scholar can give me three crushing reasons why this cannot be, yet I still hear the voice of the teacher as I read, "We can never ransom ourselves, or deliver to God the price of our life; For the ransom of our life is so great, that we should never have enough to pay it, In order to live for ever and ever, and never see the grave." How clearly these words speak to our own time, with our determination to cheat death by a multitude of increasingly costly technologies!

I suspect that I hear the voice of the teacher also in the overall theme of this psalm, which is identical to a theme echoing all through the book Ecclesiastes—the vanity of human life. The psalmist is suggesting to his contemporaries that they should censure the posturing of many in society, particularly the rich and powerful, and also the intellectual leaders.

He writes of "the wickedness of those who put their trust in their goods, and boast of their great riches." Focusing his sights on the intellectuals, he writes, "We see that the wise die also; like the dull and stupid they perish and leave their wealth to those who come after them."

As we listen, we realize that the psalmist is not dismissing wisdom itself. Nor is he denigrating possessions as such. But he is questioning the delusion of self-importance and the influence it can bring. "Such is the way of those who foolishly trust in themselves."

Now the tone changes. We are being offered a single and essential insight into human life. "Do not be envious when some become rich ... they will carry nothing away at their death." Very few of us escape the pangs of envy from time to time. The psalmist is giving us valuable advice.

Life is to be measured and evaluated from beyond itself. In the final analysis, "God will ransom my life." Thanks be to God.

❧

Consider the goals you have, and have had, for your life. Which of these goals would likely have the most lasting value for God and for others? Pray that you, and others, will form and seek goals of lasting beneficial value in the eyes of God.

Psalm 50

O Israel, I will bear witness against you;
for I am God, your God.

Soon after Alexander Solzhenitsyn came to the United States, he addressed a crowd in Harvard Square. It was the first of many addresses and articles in which he offered strong criticism of the value system not only of the Soviet Union—which was to be expected—but also of the West. His criticism came to be deeply resented.

A couple of decades later a gentler voice, that of Vaclav Havel, president of the Czech Republic, tried to carry out the same role. To what extent either voice will be heard into the future is still a question.

I suspect that the first hearing of this psalm received the same mixed response. One tries to imagine what it was like to hear these verses for the first time and to imagine the circumstances of that first hearing.

The verse, "Gather before me my loyal followers," suggests there may have been some public event. On this occasion the psalmist indulges in strong criticism of his society. In language that was natural to him and his listeners, he makes it clear that, although it is he who speaks the words, the criticism is from God. "Our God will come and will not keep silence ... to witness the judgement of his people ... God himself is judge."

There are none who escape criticism or judgement. Even those who worship faithfully are taken to task for the ease with which the ritual sacrificing of physical things has become a substitute for genuine self-offering to God. "Offer to God a sacrifice of thanksgiving and make good your vows to the Most High." Centuries have gone by, but this admonition is as valid as ever.

There is a great deal in his society that the psalmist sees as evil. Much religious life is far from genuine. "Why do you recite my statutes, and take my covenant upon your lips; Since you refuse discipline, and toss my words behind your back?" A rich list follows, including dishonesty, slander, lying, constant mutual betrayals, adultery. Then comes the warning. "Consider this well, you who forget God, lest I rend you and there be none to deliver you."

When we hear such fervent religious language today, we tend to smile indulgently, hide some embarrassment, and silently long for a little more reserve and sophistication in the speaker. Yet the disturbing question remains. If this language no longer serves in asking these very necessary questions of our public and personal life, where do we find a language that will?

One thing is certain. "Our God will come and will not keep silence."

❧

Make a list of some offerings that you give to God. Include all the care you give and things you do for your soul, the souls of others, and the good of creation. Pray that your offerings may help God to fulfill the divine purpose for you, others, and creation.

Psalm 51

Wash me through and through from my wickedness …
Make me hear of joy and gladness.

When an Eastern Orthodox Christian artist portrays the crucifixion, there will often be a human skull partly buried in the ground under the cross. The artist is communicating something important at the heart of Christian faith.

The skull belongs to Adam, the first man. The skull of Adam embodies the reality of death, faced by all humanity. The cross usually appears to be growing out of the Adam's skull. The figure of Jesus on the cross embodies life, in spite of approaching death. We are being shown a great affirmation about humanity. It involves death and in that sense defeat. But in Jesus, it also involves resurrection and, therefore, victory.

All this wrestling with our human nature echoes in this psalm. There is no attempt to deny what we are. "I know my transgressions." Unlike a modern voice, who would be concerned about his or her sense of self, the psalmist is concerned that God has been offended. "Against you only have I sinned." The first half of the psalm rails so rigorously against the self that it sounds almost obsessive to our ears: "wicked from my birth, a sinner from my mother's womb."

But as soon as these realities have been faced, there is an upsurge of "joy and gladness," a strong sense of there being "a right spirit within." Instead of being immersed in self, the writer is now ready to reach out to others, communicating the possibility of being freed from guilt. "I shall teach your ways to the wicked."

Now comes the deepest insight of the psalm. In our relationships with God and those whom we love, there is often the generous giving of possessions. We all give gifts. But deep down we know that, if there is to be a real relationship, the exchange of gifts between people is not enough. At some stage there must be the giving of the self.

What is true on the level of human relationship is equally true in our relationship with God. "I would have offered sacrifice [or gift]," but "the sacrifice of God is a troubled spirit [or self]." We are hearing one of the greatest biblical insights.

✑

Ask God to be with you. Look into yourself with kindness and gentleness. Let yourself see those things you do not like seeing, also those things you do like seeing. Offer all these things to God. Open yourself to the grace and love of God.

Psalm 52

I will give you thanks for what you have done
and declare the goodness of your name.

Some years ago a movie was made about the slow disintegration of an essentially decent and gifted person caught in the tangled web of a huge television organization. Being a national news anchorman, he speaks daily to millions. During one newscast he suggests that people express the unfocused anger they feel at society and its structures by opening a window at a certain evening hour and shouting, "I'm mad as hell, and I'm not going to take any more!"

While reading this psalm, we cannot help feeling that we are watching at least one window being opened, and hearing at least one voice shouting much the same thing.

The psalmist's opening words are an explosive release of pent-up emotion about what is happening in his world. "You tyrant, why do you boast of wickedness against the godly all day long?" This initial explosion is followed by a volley of complaint and resentment. "You plot ruin; your tongue is like a sharpened razor ... You love evil more than good ... You love all words that hurt."

Now we hear a powerful sentiment that has motivated many societies. The psalmist wishes for a decidedly different future. "Oh, that God would demolish you utterly ... and root you out of the land of the living!" Many have wished this fate for a tyrant. But the psalmist goes on to imagine the wish coming true.

He begins to imagine the world without the tyrant. He gets his listeners to think of what they would say. "The righteous ...

shall laugh … saying, 'This is the one who did not take God for a refuge.' " In a line whose meaning we can easily miss, the psalmist goes further. He assumes that God has already done—not just will do—what everyone wishes! "I will give you thanks for what you have done."

Centuries later, before the shrine of a great national liberator, another writer of lyrical prose—in his own way, a psalmist—would use the same device. Martin Luther King, Jr., wrestling not so much against a single tyrant but a great tyranny, brought the future into the present by envisioning his own children playing with others in a world where skin colour had become irrelevant.

His vision has not yet been wholly fulfilled, but there are those who will always struggle for it—those who, like the psalmist, are prepared to "trust in the mercy of God for ever and ever."

❧

Consider how people tyrannize your world. Consider how you may tyrannize the world of others. Ask God to open the hearts of all people who oppress others, that they may be led to see the suffering around them and work to bring relief.

Psalm 53

The fool has said in his heart, "There is no God" …
there is none who does any good.

The illusion that societies can survive in the long run without any common religious basis … is rightly called an illusion or self-delusion because without religion there is finally no limit to individual license except the coercive power of the law … when religious indifference becomes a mark of the public culture, we should not be surprised by the steady increase in unbridled license, by the progressive loss of consensus regarding moral and cultural values, and by social disintegration, leading, more likely than not, to tyranny and the loss of freedom.

The voice is that of Wolfhart Pannenberg from the University of Munich, giving the 1994 Erasmus Lecture. It may seem strange to begin a reflection on this psalm with such a quotation, but when we read the psalm we see why. The psalmist of more than two millennia ago and the contemporary Christian theologian are saying the same thing.

"The fool has said in his heart, 'There is no God.' " Only a few lines later the psalmist makes clear that he is not talking about one particular person. "God looks … upon us all, to see … if there is one who seeks after God." In the eyes of the psalmist, "Everyone has proved faithless."

While we can assume that faithlessness can become widespread in a society, we would find it difficult to agree with the statement:

"There is none who does good; no, not one." Even in the darkest times there are certain men and women who shine like lights because of their moral and spiritual quality. From them comes the hope that sustains others.

The psalmist makes a connection we may find difficult to see today. In typically blunt language we are told that those who deny God "are corrupt and commit abominable acts." In our society many would regard this statement as not only grossly untrue but also the height of religious arrogance.

Interestingly, one evil the psalmist seems to have in mind is the exploitation of people by the strong and unscrupulous. He speaks of "evildoers who eat up my people like bread." And this reflects what Pannenberg says above.

It is not that anyone who denies the existence of God is thereby a criminal or an evil person. Instead, as both the ancient psalmist and modern theologian are suggesting, if belief in a transcendent God is extracted from a culture, that culture runs the risk of disintegrating in the long run.

❧

Do you see signs of godless corruption in your society? Can you recall feelings, thoughts, or actions in your life in which God has seemed not present? Pray that the grace and presence of God may grow and flower in the lives of all people.

Psalm 54

Behold, God is my helper;
it is the Lord who sustains my life.

The more one reads the psalms consecutively and, therefore, becomes aware of the themes running through them, the more one realizes that their world, its assumptions and attitudes, is very different from the world we are familiar with. Consider the attitude toward enemies as expressed in this psalm.

The psalm begins with an embattled psalmist fending off his enemies and, once again, desperately pleading with God for help in the task. "Save me, O God, by your name; in your might, defend my cause." In the English translation, these four short phrases sound as if they are gasped out between blows given and received. The cry, "Hear my prayer, O God," repeated in the next psalm, emphasizes the desperation.

These enemies are by now very familiar to us. "The arrogant have risen up against me, and the ruthless have sought my life, those who have no regard for God." We cannot help wondering if, for the psalmist, people become enemies when they "have no regard for God," and if this disregard is the psalmist's justification for calling them ruthless and arrogant.

My reason for making this surmise was a news item on television within the week of writing this piece. A change of government in Israel had apparently emboldened the radically religious to exert their power to change the behaviour of those who are not practising Jews. It is quite obvious that the latter are seen as enemies who threaten a religious way of life.

With very little effort we can imagine a contemporary zealot reciting this psalm as the sirens wail and the stone he has just thrown crashes through the windshield of a passing car. Again, in the attitude of many radically religious groups, even the state itself is regarded as illegitimate and its actions are resented as intrusions into the lives of the faithful. One can hear a modern voice crying, "Render evil to those who spy on me; in your faithfulness, destroy them."

For us, the parts of this song that can be sustaining are the verses that point to God as a source of grace in times of trouble. The simple and well-proven fact is that merely asking for help and being open to the presence of God in the situation can be strengthening. "Behold, God is my helper; it is the Lord who sustains my life."

❧

We can do nothing without God. In every enterprise or difficulty, consider opening yourself to the guidance and support of God. Let yourself speak the name of God, silently or aloud. Ask God to assist others to open themselves to God's grace.

Psalm 55

Cast your burden upon the Lord,
and he will sustain you.

One of the gifts of my school years was an English teacher who had a magnificent voice and a great sense of theatre. Among the moments he made unforgettable in a classroom of easily bored youth was the scene in Shakespeare's Julius Caesar where the emperor is assassinated. In that scene the Roman senator Brutus, whom Caesar had always regarded as a friend, joins the assassins and plunges his dagger into Caesar. The dying man turns, looks at Brutus, and says, "Et tu, Brute?" — "And you, Brutus?"

There is very little in life as distressing as being betrayed by a friend. The psalmist is facing deep trouble. "My heart quakes within me, and the terrors of death have fallen upon me. Fear and trembling have come over me, and horror overwhelms me." He knows that he cannot deal with the situation much longer. "Oh, that I had wings like a dove! ... I would hasten to escape."

Once again the psalmist links his personal distress to concerns for his society. "I have seen violence and strife in the city ... corruption at her heart." Then he focuses on his current agony. "Had it been an adversary who taunted me, then I could have borne it." As if unable to believe it, he repeats the awful reality: "had it been an enemy ... then I could have hidden from him." His anguish erupts in a series of sobs. "But it was you, a man after my own heart, my companion, my own familiar friend."

Memories of good times intensify the agony. "We took sweet

counsel together, and walked with the throng in the house of God." These lines may be the most poignant in the whole Book of Psalms.

Now there is a blaze of anger! "Let death come upon them suddenly; let them go down alive into the grave." Immediately the psalmist reaches out passionately for God, who "will hear my voice … will bring me safely back from the battle."

Here, in this swiftly changing pattern of response to life's problems, lies wisdom for us all. The psalmist is willing to acknowledge and express his true feelings. Later in the psalm he returns to vilifying his betrayer, but this subsequent outburst moves him again to seek the presence of God in the situation.

The wisdom of the psalms can show us that our sorrow and hurt and anger at life—if we are prepared to acknowledge their depth—can become for us the road to the presence of God. "Cast your burden upon the Lord, and he will sustain you," says the psalmist to us.

❧

Consider someone or something that causes you trouble. Ask God to let you discover and accept your true feelings in the situation. What do your feelings tell you about yourself? Ask God to help you, and others, find grace and healing.

Psalm 56

In God, whose word I praise,
in God I trust and will not be afraid.

a most striking trait of the writer of the psalms is the vivid and immediate way he impinges on the life of the reader. We and the psalmist often meet with the suddenness of two people who round a corner and bump into each other. The psalmist is the kind of companion who hides very little. If he is depressed, afraid, angry, or ecstatic, we know it immediately.

"My enemies are hounding me ... they assault and oppress me ... there are many who fight against me." We feel his grip on our arm, hear the terror in his voice, see the fear in his eyes! But then a strange and lovely thing happens. The grip loosens. The psalmist walks away from us, as if we no longer matter. He stands a short distance off and speaks to someone neither of us can see.

His voice is calmer. His fear seems to have vanished, at least for the moment. "O Most High ... whenever I am afraid, I will put my trust in you." This person is now in the presence of a God in whom he has unshakeable trust, the kind of trust most of us envy.

We listen as he tells this God what he faces. He chats to God intimately. All the details are included in his recital, as if he is pouring out a stream of consciousness. "They damage my cause; their only thought is to do me evil. They band together ... they spy on my footsteps; because they seek my life." The thought of such implacable adversaries triggers an outburst. He implores God to do something.

The psalmist has no shadow of doubt that God knows him as a family member! "You have noted my lamentation … my tears … are they not recorded in your book?" He ends his plea to God with an assurance that is breathtaking to our modern ears. "Whenever I call upon you, my enemies will be put to flight; this I know, for God is on my side."

It is true, I think, that most of us envy this kind of sublime trust. One of the graces of spending time with the psalms is a reminder that such a level of trust can and does exist in the lives of some people.

But another thing appears in this psalm. We hear the psalmist say, "I am bound by the vow I made to you, O God; I will present to you thank-offerings." We hear the psalmist saying to us across the centuries that a healthy devotional life can be an anchor and a source of nurture for our sometimes troubled souls.

≈

How much conversation does it take to build your trust in a friend? How much conversation do you have with God? Ask God to help you increase the frequency and intimacy of your conversations with God, and to deepen your trust in God.

Psalm 57

I will call upon the Most High God,
the God who maintains my cause.

Viktor Frankl survived one of Hitler's death camps and later became a highly respected psychotherapist. He always maintained that the most important factor in the survival of his fellow prisoners was having a sense of meaning about life that called a person to strive to the utmost for survival. That very quality is evident in this psalm.

We get a sense of the depth of the psalmist's relationship with God when we hear the confident certainty that rings through his thoughts about God. "He will send from heaven and save me; he will confound those who trample upon me. God will send forth his love and faithfulness." He speaks these three statements with utmost deliberation, almost as it were through gritted teeth, with emphasis on the repeated word "will." This is more than fervent hope, certainly more than shallow optimism. It is a level of trust that we all would wish to have.

But we notice another "will," another equally determined resolution of the psalmist. "I will call upon the Most High God." Here is someone who not only looks constantly for the presence of God, but also takes care to consciously place himself in that presence again and again. In other words, it would seem that the psalmist leads a strong and disciplined devotional life.

Even more, we notice something about his devotional life that most of us find difficult. The psalmist says, "I will sing and make melody ... I myself will waken the dawn." This we can understand. He will seek the presence of God in personal moments. Most of us try to do this. But he also says, "I will confess you among the peoples, O Lord." He seems to be saying that, in the midst of his involvement in public affairs, in the comings and goings of what we would consider his professional life, he will also find time to "confess you."

Here is where this psalm offers us its particular gift of insight. Making a "space" for God in our professional lives is not only difficult, because those professional hours are so full and pressured, but even more because we do not naturally think of God as being present or available in that world of our work. The psalmist—indeed the whole Bible—asks us to reconsider this very mistaken assumption.

Two sublime images offer us a true picture of our human situation. "I lie in the midst of lions." There are always those things that threaten us. But also, God hovers over us. Our lives are lived "in the shadow of your wings."

❧

How frequently do you converse with God about the "big" concerns in your life? How frequently do you converse with God about the "little" concerns? Ask God to help you bring all your concerns large and small, all your life, to God.

Psalm 58

Do you indeed decree righteousness, you rulers?
do you judge the peoples with equity?

In the early nineteen forties, Dietrich Bonhoeffer was struggling to find effective ways to protest against the Nazi regime. He was a young Lutheran pastor who would eventually die for his participation in an unsuccessful plot to assassinate Hitler.

In his sermons and letters, many of which we still possess, Bonhoeffer frequently expressed his disgust at what he saw happening around him. We can feel his vehemence in one of his sermons, as he says, "The air that we breathe is so polluted by mistrust that it almost chokes us."

In this psalm we may be hearing the same kind of utter disgust. We have no way of knowing whether or not it was originally expressed in public. If so, its author must have been in some danger of reprisal. Ruling powers are not endeared to rhetoric such as we hear in these lines. "Do you indeed decree righteousness, you rulers? do you judge ... with equity? ... you devise evil ... deal out violence."

The psalmist's explosion of indignation leads to a spate of name-calling. "The wicked are perverse ... liars ... venomous." As if this were not enough, there follows a series of blistering maledictions. "O God, break their teeth in their mouths ... Let them vanish like water ... wither like trodden grass ... be ... like a stillborn child." All this is crowned by an image of the psalmist and his allies about to "bathe their feet in the blood of the wicked."

Language such as this is extremely powerful, especially in a culture that gave immense significance to the spoken word. Many people in our Western world feel that the freedom to indulge in extreme language, and to direct it in hatred and alienation toward government and national institutions, runs the risk of bringing about that of which it speaks.

This psalm comes to us across the centuries as a warning. Words of hatred can breed hatred. Words of alienation can generate alienation. Words of death can bring about death. We cannot remain among the righteous while bathing our "feet in the blood of the wicked," at least not in any society that we would wish to live in.

≈

Consider the maledictions expressed in your society, in both public and private life. Consider the maledictions expressed under your own breath! Ask God that all people may learn to accept their faults and to seek God's grace and healing.

Psalm 59

I will celebrate your love in the morning;
For you have become my stronghold.

From the very outset this psalm seems to be the voice of a single person. On the other hand this person seems to have a very public function. The first desperate appeal, "Rescue me from my enemies, O God," points to an individual. Yet the following phrases suggest that some danger threatens the city or nation.

The appeal, "Slay them, O God, lest my people forget," would suggest the possibility of an attacking army. If we regard this as a possible context for the psalm, then there is even greater force in the chilling image of those who "go to and fro in the evening; they snarl like dogs and run about the city." This image seems to haunt the mind of the psalmist; he repeats it with a kind of fascinated horror.

Yet even in the face of impending disaster, we hear again the extraordinary trust of the psalmist in the presence and support of God. Of his own role in whatever has led to this moment, the psalmist feels utterly justified. "Not for any offence or fault of mine … they run and prepare themselves for battle."

We are hearing what every society facing an enemy has to hear. The cause must be justified to those who are about to risk their lives for it. The enemy must be painted in the worst possible colours. The psalmist prays in public and attempts to justify his case against the enemy. "Slay them, O God … For the sins of their mouths, for the words of their lips, for the cursing and lies that they utter."

For us who read this battle song so long after the event, perhaps the most significant lines show the psalmist apparently passing from terror and loathing to something resembling serenity. "For my part I will sing of your strength; I will celebrate your love in the morning, For you have become my stronghold, a refuge in the day of my trouble."

What distinguishes these lovely lines from the usual battle song of the ancient world is the repeated use of the word "your." The king about to fight sings not of his own strength, but of the strength of his God; not of his own capacity for love, but of God's capacity for love and faithfulness. The king's stronghold and refuge is not in himself, but in his God.

In such a stance we ourselves can find grace, when the little city of our own souls is under attack.

❧

Are there times when you feel oppressed by enemies? Can you notice in yourself some of the same traits that you see in your enemies, at least to some extent? Ask God to strengthen you, and to send healing to the enemies both within and without.

Psalm 60

With God we will do valiant deeds,
and he shall tread our enemies under foot.

Soon after the last major earthquake in Los Angeles, one of the television networks got permission to go back into the damaged ground-floor apartment of an elderly Hispanic woman.

The camera followed her into the apartment, and in halting sentences she described the sequence of events. First the dishes rattled, then a cupboard toppled, then a crack opened in the wall. She told how she ran for the door, how it came off its hinges and struck her, and how she stumbled outside to the street. Then to the camera she said in an awed voice, "I knew that the earth had moved."

"O God," cries the psalmist, "You have shaken the earth and split it open; repair the cracks in it, for it totters." It may be that Jerusalem was being systematically destroyed by an enemy army. We cannot be sure. But it is obvious from the first lines that we are encountering a moment of utter disaster. "O God, you have cast us off and broken us."

The measure of despair becomes clear in the line that begs God to "take us back to you again." For the psalmist to think in terms of the absence of God indicates a grim situation indeed.

Yet if we can receive it, we have here a great spiritual gift. The psalmist is able to ascribe all aspects of this terrible event to the action of God, shocking though that action is. Notice the constant use of "you," referring to God. "You have shaken the earth and split it open ... You have made your people know hardship; you have given us wine that makes us stagger." The idea of wine is used ironically here. The psalmist is talking about the bitter wine of destruction and defeat.

Yet notice how the same God who has allowed this disaster also gives recovery. "You have set up a banner for those who fear you, to be a refuge." Later in the poem, the psalmist again complains to God, "You no longer go out, O God, with our armies." Yet almost in the same breath he assumes better possibilities in the future because of the certainty that God will help. "With God we will do valiant deeds, and [God] shall tread our enemies under foot."

The gift of this psalm is to offer us a certain quality of faith. Such faith becomes possible when we can bring ourselves to believe that all things, even the terrors of life, are within the providence of God.

❧

Can you bring yourself to believe that suffering is within the providence of God? How could your suffering and the suffering of others possibly lead to good? Ask God to give you the grace of faith and understanding in the face of this mystery.

psalm 61

O God … I call upon you … with heaviness in my heart;
set me upon the rock that is higher than I.

People in a position of power often speak and write about its essential loneliness. That wonderful and most human of popes, John XXIII, spoke about lying in bed thinking about all the problems of the church. He once said to himself, "Roncalli, what would the Pope do?" and then he sat up in bed and exclaimed, "But Roncalli, you are the Pope!"

There is in this psalm an echo of the solitariness of power, in this case kingship. We are given a glimpse of the humanity that lies behind all positions of power—the human being that carries the responsibility.

At the moment we encounter him, the king is deeply troubled. As happens so frequently in the psalms, the specific reason is not given. We get a hint that he is fearful in a way we all know. He is worried about his health. He is afraid that the end of his life may be approaching. "Add length of days to the king's life," he prays. The next line sounds almost like pleading. "Let his years extend over many generations."

If we follow his request into the next verse, we can identify immediately with his wish to live forever—the secret desire we all have in those fearful times when we face our mortality. "Let [the king] sit enthroned before God for ever." However, because we are dealing with religious poetry, the prayer here may be to live always in the presence of God. We would all do well to offer this prayer.

There is a simplicity and poignancy about this psalm. It is one of the songs we have no difficulty making our own when we need it. We are in the company of another who is feeling utterly vulnerable. "O God … I call … with heaviness in my heart." We have been there, and will be there again. "I will take refuge under the cover of your wings." Our prayer is that we too will know the shelter of those wings.

"Set me upon the rock that is higher than I," he prays. Again we echo his prayer that, when we face the sometimes fearful challenges of life, we may find available to us a stronger and more lasting power than our own meagre resources.

⟳

Are you, or is someone you know, struggling with a serious illness? Ask God to let you, or that person, grow more deeply aware of the vital presence of God, and the grace of God's comfort, strength, and power to heal—physically, emotionally, and spiritually.

Psalm 62

For God alone my soul in silence waits;
from him comes my salvation.

Somewhere in the meditations of Marcus Aurelius, that most
introspective man who was one of the later emperors of Rome,
he admits his lack of interest in the legions of his armies. In that
particular moment, he is more interested in the dark legions that
march through his dreams.

There are hints in this psalm that once again we are being ad-
mitted into the mind and soul of someone who bears high office
and therefore carries heavy and unrelenting responsibility. "How
long will you assail me to crush me, all of you together, as if you
were ... a toppling wall?"

It would seem that enemies are many. There is even the pos-
sibility of a coup or revolt, with all the deceit and treachery this
brings into a regime. "They seek only to bring me down from my
place of honour."

In the face of all these pressures, this thoughtful and essentially
devout person realizes certain truths that we all eventually discover,
especially and ironically those among us who have tasted great suc-
cess in life. "Those of high degree are but a fleeting breath, even
those of low estate cannot be trusted."

The speaker may also be thinking of things that in retrospect
he is less proud of. "In robbery take no empty pride; though wealth
increase, set not your heart upon it." One cannot help hearing

a twinge of guilt in the voice that says, "O Lord … you repay everyone according to his deeds."

We are being given what is always a privilege and a trust—access to the innermost thoughts of another human being. Such thoughts are precious also because they anticipate our own thoughts as we seek to come to terms with what we have done with our lives.

As we listen, we arrive with the psalmist at the very throne of God. Now, in the repeated admission of our companion, we know what he really wants out of life. "For God alone my soul in silence waits … In God is my safety and my honour … my strong rock and my refuge."

Even as we hear him say it, and as we move our own lips to echo it, we cannot know its full meaning. All we know and hope for is the profound truth that "steadfast love is yours, O Lord."

❧

Have you found that, when you suppress "bad" feelings, this dulls your ability to experience "good" feelings? Ask God to be with you in all your experiences, and to enfold and fill you with the power and delight of the presence of God.

Psalm 63

Your loving-kindness is better than life itself;
my lips shall give you praise.

We are alone in the presence of a king, and we are overhearing his thoughts. We might be with David himself—which would account for the sensuousness of the language—but we cannot be sure. We do know that we are with a ruler.

Those who wield power and authority tend to keep their thoughts to themselves, at least the intimations of their own inner being. It is risky to reveal oneself to all but a trusted few. Also, people who carry great responsibility tend generally to have little occasion for introspection, unless they rigorously carve out personal time. These realities make this intimate moment all the more interesting.

"O God, you are my God; eagerly I seek you; my soul thirsts for you, my flesh faints for you." The opening words are a cry, but unlike most cries in the psalms, this is an expression of—what shall we say—joy? Yes, there is "joy" in the voice, but this word doesn't fully suffice to describe what we are hearing. A passionate cry? Perhaps this gets us nearer the truth.

We are indeed listening to the cry of a lover. The language could easily be the prelude to passionate lovemaking. Though less explicit, this feeling continues into the next verse, where the lover gazes on the glory of the beloved. Later in the song we hear him say, "My mouth praises you with joyful lips."

We realize that we are in the company of someone who loves

God with the passion that most of us reserve for human loving. The moment we realize this, we have received a gift from the poet. He has reminded us that most people's relationship with God is a poor and pathetic thing compared with what we are hearing in these lines.

"I remember you upon my bed … For you have been my helper." How very seldom we think about God in this way, recalling the moments in our lives when we discovered that a strength beyond our own was made available to us; when we were conscious, perhaps for only a fleeting moment, that a presence other than ourselves made it possible for us to pull through.

For such moments in life we need to give thanks. "For you have been my helper, and under the shadow of your wings I will rejoice."

〜

Can you recall a time when you were hard-pressed, but you showed energy and resourcefulness beyond your expectations? Give thanks for the grace of God in that situation, and ask that you may always be inspired to seek God's help.

Psalm 64

The righteous will rejoice in the Lord
and put their trust in him.

In the world of the psalmist, not much thought is given to "keeping a stiff upper lip," as the English are apt to say. Instead, people express what they feel. If they are angry, they vent it. If they are afraid, they let it be known far and wide. If they have a complaint against God, they cry out their indignation to the heavens!

"Hear my voice, O God, when I complain." There is no apology for this approach to God, no admission that the speaker might resemble a small child who feels that only his or her complaint matters. Admittedly, as we continue to listen to the psalmist, we become aware that this is no frivolous matter. It sounds like a life-or-death situation. And yet ....

"Protect my life from fear of the enemy." Notice the words "fear of." I cannot help wondering whether this oft-repeated plea of the psalm writer is about enemies or about fear of enemies. Are these enemies sometimes imagined, what we today would call projections? We get a hint of this in the very next phrase. "Hide me from the conspiracy of the wicked."

Again we wonder about these wicked people and their conspiracy, real or imagined. "They sharpen their tongue ... aim their bitter words ... plan how they may hide their snares." As yet, there is no actual attack, no physical presence. Are we hearing from someone threatened by external danger or struggling with inner fear?

Of course, we can never know. As the psalmist says, "The

human mind and heart are a mystery." But even if it were true that this threat exists only in the mind of the poet, it is significant for us that he seeks refuge with God. With God fear can be turned to confidence and assurance. "God will loose an arrow at them … He will make them trip over their tongues."

So often the message of the psalms—which comes to our less-believing age with special poignancy—speaks of a source of grace beyond the self, beyond human relationships, beyond community. All these things are so valued in our age, and so precious and necessary. And within them and beyond them, there is God. "The righteous will rejoice in the Lord and put their trust in him, and all who are true of heart will glory."

&

Consider a fear that oppresses you. How much of the cause of this fear lies outside you? How much of the cause lies inside you? Ask God to help you face and understand your fear, and to let there be healing for the cause of your fear.

Psalm 65

Happy are they whom you ... draw to your courts ...
Awesome things will you show us.

It is difficult for us to imagine how much the temple in Jerusalem meant to a Jewish believer in the psalmist's time. We have sacred shrines today—St. Peter's in Rome, Canterbury Cathedral—but there is no comparison between our attitude to these great cathedrals and that of a Jew to the temple. Before its destruction in AD 70, we could almost say that the temple was Judaism.

"They whom you choose and draw to your courts ... will be satisfied by the beauty ... of your temple." We can assume that the psalmist, either in fact or in imagination, is standing in the temple itself. But we are struck by the direction his thoughts now take.

Suddenly he is soaring across the world. Suddenly the God of this temple has become the "hope of all the ends of the earth and of the seas that are far away." Suddenly we are being made aware of "those who dwell at the ends of the earth."

Now we find ourselves thinking in lyrical terms about the cycle of the seasons and the fertility of the earth. The psalmist is ascribing every aspect of these timeless processes to God. "You visit the earth and water it ... You prepare the grain ... You drench the furrows ... You crown the year with your goodness."

An experience that begins in a particular building in a particular city has somehow enlarged the mind and imagination of the worshipper to encompass the whole of humanity and the whole planet.

The God who is being worshipped in this place cannot be bound by the building or by the words said and sung in its rituals.

As Christians, particularly in the West, we need to ask if this universal quality can be captured by our forms of worship. Can our liturgies give us a vision of the planet, of all the processes of nature, now under such threat? Can our worship make us aware of the infinitely varied throng of humanity, beginning to form a multicultural world? Do we conceive this God, whom we worship in Jesus Christ, as being the source to whom "shall all flesh come," and the "Hope of all the ends of the earth"?

Somehow Judaism with its temple was, on the one hand, sufficiently particular and defined to give its people a strong identity and, on the other hand, entirely capable of giving them a song for the planet and the universe. We need to learn such a song today, and we need to be heard singing it.

❧

Is there some building or place in your life that embodies and reflects vital aspects of life for you? Is this place hospitable to the grace and presence of God? Ask God to bless and inhabit the temple of your life, and to fill it with goodness, peace, and joy.

Psalm 66

Come now and see the works of God,
how wonderful he is in his doing toward all people.

Perhaps all cultures tend to hear two voices calling them in diametrically opposite directions. One voice calls people to put their energies into forming their own national identity, strengthening the institutions of their country, celebrating their own culture. The other voice calls them to play a part, large or small, on the world stage, to contribute their gifts to many cultures, to participate in the global community. Certainly these two voices have always existed in Judaism. We hear both voices in the psalms.

"I will enter your house with burnt-offerings and will pay you my vows ... I will offer you sacrifices of fat beasts." This language depicts what we might call the cult aspect of the psalmist's religion. When we attend our parish church to celebrate eucharist, we are joining in a cultic activity, and it is proper to do so. But it is important to be clear about the purpose of our participation. Sometimes it can be for personal reasons. We are seeking guidance or grace for something we must deal with.

It seems as if, on this occasion, the psalmist is facing a personal issue. "[I] will pay you my vows, which I promised ... when I was in trouble ... in truth God has heard me ... not rejected my prayer, nor withheld his love from me." The psalmist had known some trouble, had prayed to God, and had received grace. For this he is giving thanks by sacrificing in the temple because he believes, as we do, that God "holds our souls in life."

But we can't help noticing how far beyond the personal he goes in his prayers and praises. He thinks about incidents in the life of his own people. "[God] turned the sea into dry land ... tried us just as silver is tried ... brought us out into a place of refreshment." The psalmist then unrolls a kind of mental map of the world and sees it all as God's domain. "Be joyful in God, all ye lands ... Come now and see ... how wonderful [God] is ... his eyes keep watch over the nations."

The lesson of this psalm applies to our own cultic activity. If our worship is to remain healthy and creative, it must always move beyond our personal concerns—totally valid though they be—and reach out to include the community we worship in, the larger community of the church, and the largest community of all—humanity itself. Our worship calls to us: "Come now and see the works of God, how wonderful he is in his doing toward all people."

᠁

In your personal meditations and communal worship, when you offer your concerns to God, consider the concerns of others—family, friends, community, country, world—which may be similar to yours, and offer these concerns to God for them also.

Psalm 67

May God give us his blessing,
and may all the ends of the earth stand in awe of him.

If we bring our imaginations into play to propose a setting for this psalm, we may gain a worthwhile insight about the psalmist, his people, and their religion. There is a line in this psalm that might indicate where and when it was first sung. "The earth has brought forth her increase."

Perhaps the loveliest time in Israel—for that matter, the loveliest time in any land—is when the cycle of the year brings again the fruits of the earth. The people are gathered in the temple, and they are thanking God for the blessings once again received. They are asking the God who has given the harvest to bless them also in other ways. "May God, our own God, give us his blessing."

Notice how they describe the source of their blessings. God is "our own God," they sing. We might expect such language to limit their thinking, and their prayer life as a people, to their own concerns. But the very opposite is true. Certainly they continually bring the concerns of Israel before their God. But they never stop there. This is what is so important, and it is what we need to hear clearly from this and many other psalms.

Referring to God as "our own God" never deludes Israel into thinking that God is limited to them or that the concerns of God end with them. Certainly they believe passionately that they are the concern of God, but they do not imagine they are the only concern.

"May God be merciful to us and bless us." So begins the song. But the psalmist takes only a moment, a single verse, to hurl us out among the nations. "Let your ways be made known upon earth, your saving health among all nations … let all the peoples praise you … Let the nations be glad."

Then the psalmist drops a statement so casually and with such assurance that we may easily miss its huge claim. "You … guide all the nations upon earth." Israel is not claiming here to rule all nations in the name of God. Their claim is made on behalf of God, not Israel. They could not conceive of God as being less than universal.

Perhaps we need to ask ourselves if our concepts of God are as large and as inclusive as that of the people who gave us this psalm.

≈

Use your knowledge of religion and your own intuition to formulate a description of God. What are the most intimate characteristics of God you can imagine? What are the most cosmic characteristics? Ask God to guide and inspire you in your search to know God.

Psalm 68

Blessed be the Lord day by day,
the God of our salvation, who bears our burdens.

There is something really exciting about a well-organized parade. A modest community effort, with local organizations and local bands, can be fascinating to watch. But a huge parade, with representatives and images and music of a nation's life, can be thrilling.

"They see your procession, O God, your procession into the sanctuary ... The singers go before, musicians follow after ... maidens playing upon the hand-drums ... the princes of Judah ... of Zebulon and Naphtali." The psalmist is deeply moved as he attends some special occasion in the temple, and watches a liturgical procession depicting a cross-section of the national life of his people. This experience triggers a series of reflections on the nature of the God who is being honoured.

Through the rest of these verses, the psalmist pours out images conveying his understanding of the nature of God. We begin to see two streams of images. The first depicts a God of great power. "The chariots of God are twenty thousand, even thousands of thousands ... God shall crush the heads of his enemies ... Trample down those who lust after silver, scatter the peoples that delight in war ... [God] sends forth ... his mighty voice."

These images of the power of God do not all come together, but are woven into the texture of the whole psalm. And interwoven between them is a very different set of images of the same God.

This God has chosen the mountain on which the temple stands "for his resting place."

It would seem that this God of power is also a God of stillness, reflection, and contemplation. This God is "like a dove whose wings are covered with silver"—a God who seeks peace. This God is "father of orphans, defender of widows" and "bears our burdens." This God has "made provision for the poor" and "gives the solitary a home and brings forth prisoners into freedom."

This psalm has given us two sets of attributes for the nature of God. We have been shown a powerful God and a moral God. For the psalmist these attributes paint the portrait of the one God. May we keep this portrait always before us!

❧

This psalm assigns ultimate power and morality to God. Consider some other attributes of God that you can infer from your own life, the lives of others, and the life of the universe. Let your spirit reach out to this God, who is All in One.

Psalm 69

I looked … for comforters, but I could find no one …
your help, O God, will lift me up on high.

One cannot help wondering if the seeds of the Twelve Steps pro-
gram—which has been so valuable for so many suffering various
addictions—were fertilized from the reading of the psalms.

Again and again in these poems the writer describes some
agony he is suffering. We are given a vivid portrait that shows every
detail—almost nothing is held back. Lower and lower we descend
with the psalmist, until we arrive at bedrock. Then a beautiful thing
happens. We watch as someone reaches out to God, receives grace,
and begins the journey back to life.

"Save me, O God, for the waters have risen up to my neck."
This cry could not be more stark and more human. There follows
a litany of utter misery. "I am sinking … there is no firm ground
… with my crying; my throat is inflamed." This last detail suggests
a terrible loneliness. No one is responding. Then we hear that "my
eyes have failed from looking for my God." For the psalmist, or
for anyone in his culture, to admit the seeming absence of God is
a measure of the desperate state of that suffering soul.

Now the situation is described. It looks as if the psalmist has
been foolish in some action linked with money. We can only guess
at the specific meaning of these lines: "Must I then give back what
I never stole? O God, you know my foolishness, and my faults are
not hidden from you."

The appeals to God for help rise to a crescendo. "Save me …

do not let me sink ... do not let the Pit shut its mouth upon me." There is another admission of desperate loneliness. "I looked for sympathy, but there was none, for comforters, but I could find no one."

At this point the psalmist lashes out in anger. Nothing is too bad to wish on his enemies. "Let their eyes be darkened ... give them continual trembling in their loins." This spasm of anger culminates in a scream. "Let them be wiped out of the book of the living." But even as the scream is still ringing in our ears, there is a surprising change.

A corner has been turned. The anger seems to have engendered an ability to take charge again. The psalmist still suffers. "As for me, I am afflicted and in pain." But now he finds a source of grace. The word "will" is repeated like a chorus. "Your help, O God, will lift me up ... I will praise the name of God ... I will proclaim [God's] greatness ... God will save."

We watch, amazed and joyful, as a soul returns from death to life, and we realize that some day it could be us.

<hr>

Do you know anyone in extreme suffering or deprivation? Are you aware of any group, in your local community or the global community, in extreme suffering or deprivation? Ask God to be with them and relieve them, to strengthen and comfort them.

Psalm 70

You are my helper and my deliverer;
O Lord, do not tarry.

Since we have no way of knowing the circumstances of those who wrote the psalms, frequently also we do not know what problems the psalmist may be referring to. His troubles are left to our imagination. But this very lack of definition has allowed people to come to these psalms for centuries and to identify their own troubles with those of the psalmist.

"Be pleased, O God, to deliver me; O Lord, make haste to help me." There is not a single soul who has not had cause to express this cry at some time. It is significant that for centuries, as millions of Christians have begun their daily worship in the tradition of *The Book of Common Prayer*, they have used this very petition, changed only slightly: "O God, make speed to save us," with the response, "O Lord, make haste to help us."

In the words "make speed" and "make haste" there is an implicit admission of our human vulnerability. We are saying that we cannot hold on forever without help. We know that, within ourselves, there are resources we have received from God, but there are times when these resources seem unavailable to us and we are no longer able to cope.

The psalmist obviously has enemies, but in this psalm they do not seem to be life threatening. He speaks of "those who seek my life," but his other remarks suggest that he is referring not to physical danger, but perhaps something like character assassination or professional sabotage.

If he is a teacher or a priest of the temple, he could be facing the vicious politics that trouble the worlds of academia and, at times, the church. If he is a government bureaucrat or business executive, he could be under siege from competitors outside or inside the organization. There are those who seem to "take pleasure in my misfortune" and say, " 'Aha!' and gloat."

But now he tries to think of those who are not like his enemies. "Let those who love your salvation say for ever, 'Great is the Lord!' " He may imagine himself among such people, feeling at home with them, being supported by them. Although he still faces problems—"As for me, I am poor and needy"—he has moved beyond his foes and into a circle of friends. He is prepared to presume that help is available. "You are my helper and my deliverer."

Once again the psalms sing their great repeated song, assuring us of God's presence in all circumstances of life.

❧

When you are threatened by foes, within or beyond yourself, ask God to give you strength and to send them healing. When you are supported by friends, within or beyond yourself, ask God to give you gratitude and to send them blessing.

Psalm 71

O God, be not far from me …
you have done great things;
who is like you, O God?

Alfred Lord Tennyson wrote some haunting lines in which he pictures the aged hero Ulysses expressing his frustration and fears about aging. In spite of feeling old and beyond adventuring, Ulysses is determined to make one more voyage. He insists that he is ready "to strive, to seek, to find, and not to yield."

In this psalm we hear some very natural worries about aging and its insecurities. The gift of these verses lies in the psalmist's conviction that the presence of God dwells in all the experiences of life. Because God has been "my confidence since I was young," this same God is now the foundation for hope.

At the same time, in the wonderfully realistic way of the psalms, there is no suggestion that such hope comes easily. In the statement, "I have become a portent to many," we hear something that frequently distresses the aged. Because our culture wishes to deny aging and the intimations of mortality that it implies, we can sometimes detect in the eyes of others a distaste, a wish to distance themselves from the one who has aged. For this and other reasons, we hear in the psalm the different moods that sweep over our aging.

We can hear the courage and confidence of "you are my crag and my stronghold." But we can also hear the pathetic plea, "Do not cast me off in my old age." There can be moments when this plea moves into an even greater sense of desperation and helplessness. "Come quickly to help me, O my God."

In our culture the psalmist's concerns may seem somewhat overdone. All this lamentation and pleading may seem to our ears like excessive self-revelation. But as so often in the psalms, we eventually see the reason. After the psalmist has poured out his sense of misery about aging, he can then take hold of himself. There is a last cry, "now that I am old and gray-headed, O God, do not forsake me," and then it is done with.

Now as we listen, a very beautiful thing happens. "You will restore my life … You strengthen me more and more; you enfold and comfort me." This change of mood brings with it a recovery of will. "I will praise you … I will sing to you … I play to you … my tongue will proclaim your righteousness." Age has discovered its vocation to celebrate both life that has been lived and life that is yet to be lived.

❧

Ask God to help those who care for the elderly, to give them strength, compassion, and understanding. Ask God to help the elderly, to give them peace, comfort, and fulfilment. May people of all ages know the grace and presence of God.

Psalm 72

Give the king your justice, O God ...
That he may rule your people righteously.

At the inauguration of an American president or the crowning of a British monarch, the new head of state normally makes certain promises. Although phrased differently, depending on the person assuming high office, these assurances always have a particular similarity. The new rulers pledge their integrity and their concern for all the people rather than a particular element of society. In a word, they promise to be good heads of state.

There is another constant element in their promises. Always they acknowledge that they stand before a higher court than that of the society itself. They hold authority under God.

When we ask where these customs came from, we are led to the biblical tradition. This psalm provides one of the most explicit statements about authority in a society. "Give the king your justice ... and your righteousness." But only for one purpose and under one condition, that he "rule your people righteously ... with justice."

The people are not the possession of the ruler. They are "your [God's] people." Millennia before we will hear of a "preferential option for the poor," the psalms draw our attention to "the lowly ... the poor ... the needy." Only in a regime that cares for these sectors of society will there be "abundance of peace." The moral integrity of such a society is its strength, making it a blessing to other nations.

Christians know that these principles were embodied in our

Lord, but we also expect to see them in those to whom we give authority. We look for these principles in the institution of our country. They will never be perfectly embodied in any human being or institution. But our never-ending hope of finding them in public life is a reflection of our Advent hope in Jesus Christ.

∞

To what extent do rulers in your society seek God's guidance in their decision-making? To what extent do you seek God's guidance in your decision-making? Pray that people in any kind of authority may be led to seek the guidance and support of God.

Psalm 73

Whom have I in heaven but you?
and having you I desire nothing upon earth.

John Gay, an eighteenth-century writer with a sharp and witty tongue, once said, "Fools may our scorn, not envy, raise. For envy is a kind of praise." Gay was astute in that observation. I may detest the person I envy, but in or about them I see something desirable for me.

The psalmist has just emerged from a period of envy, and only now realizes how deeply it had entered into him. "My feet had nearly slipped; I had almost tripped and fallen." He is quite honest about this experience. "I envied the proud and saw [presumably with envy] the prosperity of the wicked."

The psalmist goes on to speak of the very rich as we all do in our envious moments. Like us, he projects into the world of the rich those elements that he thinks must be present. "They suffer no pain, and their bodies are sleek and sound." He sounds as if he has been reading endless issues of the New Yorker, and has been devilishly impressed by the svelte advertising!

Then comes the conviction that wealth must of necessity indicate great wickedness. They "wrap their violence around them like a cloak … their hearts overflow with wicked thoughts … they plan oppression … their evil speech runs through the world." These statements are not necessarily accurate. It is true that wickedness has made many people very rich. It is not true that the rich are necessarily wicked.

But the psalmist's next observation is indeed valid. "The people turn to them and find in them no fault." To prove the truth of this saying, we have only to think of the cult of celebrity in our own time. The more vapid or licentious the life of a celebrity, the more he or she seems to fascinate us.

But the psalmist eventually loses his envy. This may have happened during an occasion of worship. He realizes that to be rich does not make life perfect. As is so often true in his culture, his language is exaggerated. The rich are not necessarily "cast … down in ruin … [bound to] come to destruction … and perish from terror" as he says, but they are prone to all that being human entails.

What the psalmist has discovered is what we all need to discover. Whether rich or poor, we cannot live our lives without meaning. And ultimate meaning derives from God. At the end of the day, we will all echo a lovely line from this psalm. "Whom have I in heaven but you? and having you I desire nothing upon earth."

❧

Do you detect any envy in yourself? Ask God to help you value your own God-given gifts, and to release you from envy. Do you detect any envy in your world? Ask God to help all people discover life's ultimate value and meaning in God.

Psalm 74

God is my king from ancient times,
victorious in the midst of the earth.

To read this psalm is to share firsthand in the single most terrible experience that the psalmist's generation experienced. The temple and the surrounding city, the dwelling place of God and the centre of the world for them, was destroyed by the Roman army in a frenzy of fire and butchery. "The enemy has laid waste everything in your sanctuary … roared in your holy place."

This psalm is a great cry that can be summed up in one agonized word: Why? "O God, why have you utterly cut us off?" To the psalmist what has happened is incomprehensible. The people have always believed themselves to be in a covenant relationship with God. "Remember your congregation that you purchased long ago." Now every aspect of their national life is gone. The people have no guidance, no direction. "There are no signs for us to see … no prophet left.'"

So why is God allowing these things to happen? The psalmist asks a question that, in moments of agony and terror, humanity will ask until the end of time. "Why do you draw back your hand? … Yours is the day, yours also the night; you established the moon and the sun." The tone passes into a weary pleading, as if the singer has no more energy for this agonized dialogue with God. "Do not hand over the life of your dove to wild beasts; never forget the lives of your poor."

Yet, as always in the extraordinary resilience of Judaism, we begin to hear intimations of a faith that cannot be broken even by this ultimate catastrophe. "Look upon your covenant [O God]." The implication is that the bond with God still stands in spite of everything that has taken place.

"Arise, O God, maintain your cause; remember how fools revile you." The psalmist is not going to indulge in such foolishness. For him, and for his people, God is always there. Given this unshakeable faith, there is meaning in whatever happens. If God is God, then there must be meaning!

Trust in God is adamant. "God is my king from ancient times, victorious in the midst of the earth." This faith that stands like a rock is the psalmist's greatest gift to us.

❧

How can you develop a strong and stable trust in God? Train yourself to consult God at all times and for all things—good and bad, small and large, hopes and fears, joys and sorrows. Listen always for God's counsel in all areas of your life.

Psalm 75

Though the earth and all its inhabitants are quaking,
I will make its pillars fast.

When people in the far future look back at our times, they may decide that the greatest struggle for Christian faith revolved around the issue of judgement. There is an absolute clash between the attitudes of our culture and that of the Bible. By and large our culture avoids judging. The idea that there is a hierarchy of values is anathema to the contemporary mind. We have only to read this psalm to hear the clash of cultures.

The psalm begins with a burst of thanksgiving. "We give you thanks, O God, we give you thanks … [for] all your wonderful deeds." God's response to this seems surprising. " 'I will appoint a time,' says God, 'I will judge with equity.' " If we rushed up to someone with effusive thanks for the wonderful things they had done for us, and they turned and said, "I'm taking you to court," we would be quite taken aback!

God continues to speak of the inevitability of judgement. The wicked are warned of their pride. In an ancient image from Judaic culture, God offers the wicked a cup of judgement, "full of spiced and foaming wine," which they must drink. We are reminded of Jesus' use of this image of a cup, more than once, to express how God can test or judge us, sometimes in terrible ways.

But now we begin to see what the psalmist is saying to us about the judgement of God and the necessity for it. There is a clue in the verse, "Though the earth and all its inhabitants are quaking, I will make its pillars fast." Life lived under judgement is life lived with foundation! If this kind of language is difficult for us, perhaps we can suggest the same idea by saying that we live in a moral universe.

Morality may change over time for valid reasons, but as long as humans are human there will be a moral sense, and therefore we will continue to be held responsible for our actions. This is what the psalmist means when he writes, "[God] shall break off all the horns of the wicked; but the horns of the righteous shall be exalted."

Our understanding of such terms as "wicked" or "righteous" may change, but we will continue to make such distinctions, because consequences will always flow from human actions, whatever language we use to describe either the actions or the consequences.

Are there values you would consider timeless? Are there values you would consider capable of change, according to epoch and culture? Ask God to increase your compassion and inform your conscience to discern the difference.

Psalm 76

The earth was afraid and was still;
When God rose up to judgement.

After the Battle of Agincourt, when the slaughter was over and the weary but victorious King Henry V was surveying the battlefield, he was alternately exultant about the victory and appalled by the cost of it. As if he wanted to deflect responsibility from himself and place it on the shoulders of God, he gave orders that "Non Nobis" be sung as an anthem. "Not unto us, O Lord, not unto us, but unto thy name give glory."

This psalm is a kind of "Non Nobis." "In Judah is God known … he broke the flashing arrows … and the weapons of battle … both horse and rider lie stunned." Obviously, Israel has been victorious in battle, with a resulting release of tension and general euphoria. "How glorious you are! more splendid than the everlasting mountains!"

In all this celebration we detect what may be a puzzling assumption. While the victory belongs to the army and people of Israel, the conquest in a deeper sense belongs to God. Today we would have qualms about such assumptions. We would baulk at the claim that God endorses the horror and murder of battle, and recoil from celebrating our victories with language that makes this claim.

But there is always a message in scriptures such as this psalm, although it may not be obvious at first. We get an indication in the verse, "From heaven you pronounced judgement." We hear it repeated at a later stage, "When God rose up to judgement."

The concept of God as the source of ultimate judgement makes all the difference in claiming that God gave Israel the victory. Because their God is a God of judgement, Israel could also have been defeated—as it was many times. The psalmist and his contemporaries believed that victory depended on their society being "righteous" or, we might say, "right with God."

This psalm is saying to us across the centuries that the real strength of a society depends on the quality of its moral life or the state of its soul.

❧

Being "right with God" is living according to the will of God. Consider how people have interpreted the will of God differently in different times and situations. Pray that all people may be moved to seek the will of God in the present time and situation.

Psalm 77

[O God] I will meditate on all your acts
and ponder your mighty deeds.

When we look at the various elderly men who appear in some of Shakespeare's plays, we begin to suspect that the playwright had a fear of old age. At one of the many pathetic moments in *King Lear*, the king says, "I am a very foolish fond old man, Fourscore and upwards, not an hour more nor less; And, to deal plainly, I fear I am not in my perfect mind."

This particular fear—of being no longer in control of one's life—is the theme of this psalm. The psalmist is now elderly. He is having difficulty sleeping. "My hands were stretched out by night … I am restless … You will not let my eyelids close." Such sleeplessness almost always attracts the fears and anxieties of the night. They grow huge and threatening. "I ponder, and my spirit faints."

Now memories flood the mind of the psalmist. Faces and voices of the past walk across the night hours between sleep and wakefulness. "I consider the days of old; I remember the years long past." He remembers when he was young and full of energy, confident of time as a friend instead of the enemy it has become.

All these thoughts rise to a crescendo in four agonized questions that are really one question. "Will the Lord cast me off for ever? will he no more show his favour? Has his loving-kindness come to an end for ever? … Has God forgotten to be gracious?" Clearly we hear the cries of battle with the demons of aging that we all wage, or will wage.

The turning point of such thoughts, like the dawn itself, is a mingling of light and shadow. It comes between the two verses, "I said, 'My grief is this: the right hand of the Most High has lost its power,' " and "I will remember the works of the Lord ... and ponder your mighty deeds." This is the moment when the sleepless psalmist escapes from the prison cell of introspection and focuses on the reality of God beyond himself.

A series of images proclaims God's saving acts. "God ... works wonders ... redeemed your people ... the skies thundered ... lit up the world ... led your people like a flock."

Again we have been offered the choice given to us so often in the psalms, the ultimate reality of God rather than a fascination with our narrow self as the focus of our thoughts day or night. O God, "I will meditate on all your acts."

❧

If you lie awake at night and fears and anxieties assail you, open yourself to God. Share your fears and anxieties with God. Ask God to give you understanding, courage, and trust. Ask God to help all those plagued with worry in the night.

Psalm 78

That which we have heard and known ...
we will not hide from their children.

Not long before the implosion of the Soviet Union, Neil Postman wrote, in an article in *The Atlantic*,

> Nations ... require stories and may die for lack of a believable one. In America we have told ourselves for two hundred years that our experiment in government is part of God's plan ... In the Soviet Union they have told themselves that their experiment is part of history's plan ... I have the impression that neither of these two nations believes its story now—and woe unto both if they do not find some other.

This psalm is a magnificent telling of the story of the people of Israel. "I will declare the mysteries of ancient times ... what our forefathers have told us ... We will recount to generations to come." This story is about to be told for the most important reason in the world—to ensure the memory of the people, "that the generations to come might know, and the children yet unborn." The reason for ensuring this memory is "that they might put their trust in God," so that the nation will have a solid inner core to keep it strong.

To hear these verses about preserving the memory of a people is to realize the importance of this psalm for us today. The idea that our society might have its own story is widely challenged. To try to tell this story is to be dismissed with contempt.

The power of the psalmist's telling resides in those verses beginning with the word "but." Each time he recalls the actions of God on behalf of the nation, he introduces a caveat. "But they went on sinning ... But they did not stop their craving ... But they flattered him with their mouths and lied to him with their tongues ... But they tested the Most High God and defied him."

This list provides a stern comment on human willfulness and recalcitrance. Yet in spite of everything, God refuses to give up this people. "Many times he held back his anger." Here is the heart of the matter—the limitless mercy of God toward human waywardness and depravity.

We desperately need this vision of God in a world of Rwandas and Bosnias and Gazas, to mention only one kind of contemporary darkness. We could add the lengthening list of threats to life, as we know it, on this planet—most, if not all, of our own doing and within our hands to address.

It is so easy to assume that the modern world has forfeited its claim to being the creation of a loving God. It is so vital not to make this assumption, but to believe that God has "built his sanctuary like the heights of heaven, like the earth which he founded for ever."

❧

Consider the benefits to citizens in valuing the history of their nation. Consider the benefits to you in valuing the history of your life. Pray that all people may learn to value their corporate and personal past, and to seek the guidance of God for their future.

Psalm 79

We are your people and the sheep of your pasture;
we will give you thanks for ever.

They were brothers, probably from Rome. They found themselves preaching in Gaul, until they were unlucky enough to get swept up in one of the third century's periods of vicious persecution. They may have fled to England, but in the end they were martyred.

One of the brothers was given a timeless memorial by Shakespeare because the battle of Agincourt was fought on his feast day. His name was Crispin; his brother's name Crispinian. One more piece of information about them—as they prepared to die, they reflected on, and recited, this psalm. We can see why they chose it. The psalmist is crying out in desperation.

For the brothers who were about to know a martyr's death, the citadel of the new faith was being stormed. For the psalmist before them, Jerusalem was laid waste in one of the countless attacks on the city. "They have made Jerusalem a heap of rubble." The vivid images suggest the writing of an eyewitness. "The bodies of your servants as food for the birds ... blood like water on every side of Jerusalem, and there was no one to bury them."

Even in abject defeat and utter devastation, the psalmist and his contemporaries find meaning in all this seeming meaninglessness by turning to God. The defeat means that God is angry. The reason for God's anger must lie in the behaviour of God's people. "How long will you be angry, O Lord? ... Help us, O God our Saviour."

In this complete faith in a God who plays a crucial role in all events, good and bad, there is no contradiction in believing that God is the source of both the disaster and the grace to recover from it. The people know there is a reason for defeat. They do not flinch from accepting that the fault lies in themselves. "Remember not our past sins; let your compassion be swift to meet us."

If confession is made and there is genuine national repentance, then God can easily bring good from all of this agony. Nothing can change the covenant relationship between Israel and their God. "We are your people and the sheep of your pasture." In spite of any disaster "we will give you thanks for ever."

We post-modern people may smile, but as we see our own society under siege, it is possible that our amusement is tinged with more than a little envy.

✎

Recall a disaster in the world. Recall a difficult happening in your life. In both these events, what part was played by human will, and what part by divine law? Ask God to guide you and all people to seek the will of God in all aspects of life.

Psalm 80

O God ... [we will] never turn away from you;
give us life, that we may call upon your name.

One of the salutary lessons we learn from reading the psalms is the extent to which the history of Israel is bound up with violence and suffering. The holocaust has captured our attention in recent decades. So we can easily forget that, though it was by far the most terrible chapter of Jewish suffering, the holocaust has been preceded by countless other agonies.

"How long will you be angered despite the prayers of your people? ... Restore us, O Lord God of hosts." The words and the tone are familiar. An enemy army has wreaked havoc—city walls destroyed, the countryside pillaged, captives taken into servitude, loved ones killed. Now people are desperately trying to make sense of it all and to pick up the pieces of their lives. The names of the tribes—Ephraim, Benjamin, and Manasseh—tell us that this happened in the northern reaches of the country.

In the midst of the desolation we hear the voice of the psalmist. "You have brought a vine out of Egypt ... You prepared the ground for it ... stretched out its tendrils." He is struggling to find meaning in the meaningless. Ever since he was a child, he has been taught that God formed this people, brought them out of slavery, and gave them a country. Why does God now afflict them? The psalmist is asking one of the oldest human questions.

Continuing to think of his country as a vine planted by God, he asks, "Why have you broken down its wall?" Since time began, there has been no simple answer to this kind of question. But it is important for us to hear what the psalmist says in response. "Turn now, O God … behold and tend this vine; preserve what your right hand has planted."

There is not the slightest turning away from God because of what has happened. The psalmist asserts this categorically. "We will never turn away from you." Instead there is an obvious determination to turn to God as the source of aid to rebuild the devastation and to find meaning in the agony.

So sure are these people that God is their source of grace for the future that they reiterate their conviction like a recurring chorus. "Restore us, O Lord God of hosts; show the light of your countenance, and we shall be saved." Our response to this psalm is a prayer that we ourselves may find that quality of trust in God.

❦

Ask God to give people strength to consider their pain, to search their souls, and to accept the mystery of their suffering. Ask God to guide people to seek and trust the will of God. Include yourself in these considerations and prayers.

Psalm 81

Blow the ram's-horn at the new moon,
and at the full moon, the day of our feast.

In a large liturgical gathering we become aware that something is happening in ourselves. As the processions advance in their stately lines, as the music and the singing gather in strength and intensity, as the sense of occasion communicates itself to everyone, something happens. The crowd of individuals becomes a single organism. Institutional problems and issues are forgotten. A great pride, even joy, begins to surface.

"Sing with joy to God our strength ... raise a loud shout ... Raise a song ... sound the timbrel ... Blow the ram's-horn." Immediately we identify with the energy and the enthusiasm of this moment. We are in the temple on a feast day, perhaps the feast of trumpets at new moon, or the feast of tabernacles at full moon. Somewhere in this throng stands the psalmist, caught up in the beauty and power of the worship he loves and shares with those around him.

But this moment of worship also challenges him. The voice of God comes to mind and raises some uncomfortable issues. The people are reminded of their escape from captivity. "'I eased his shoulder from the burden ... I saved you ... I answered you.'" But they have responded with a fragile faith. "'My people did not hear my voice, and Israel would not obey me.'" Their vacillating relationship with God has always brought consequences, sometimes terrible consequences. "I gave them over to the stubbornness of their hearts, to follow their own devices."

Now the psalmist's impression of the voice of God changes. Warning becomes pleading. The people are told about the benefits of a faithful relationship with God. "'Oh, that my people would listen to me! … I should soon subdue their enemies."

As we know, all this reflection takes place in the context of festival worship. These great liturgical celebrations can lift us beyond the ordinary concerns of life, not denying such realities but allowing us to thrill to a greater vision. We feel a solidarity with others, a confidence in who we are, a hope for the future. For a moment we feel ourselves to be fed "with the finest wheat" and satisfied "with honey from the rock."

᙭

Make a list of some occasions when you have enjoyed wholesome celebration with others, in both personal and communal gatherings. Thank God for the gift of celebration. Ask for God's grace in all future achievements and celebrations.

Psalm 82

God takes his stand in the council of heaven;
he gives judgement in the midst of the gods.

It is easy to forget the long journey the human mind has taken toward the concept of a single universal God. For Christians the road winds through the centuries of Jewish thinking, imagining, and searching. Even on this road there are times when the concept becomes clearer than at other times.

For centuries the lesser gods remained on the periphery of human thinking, always offering their seductions, and sometimes succeeding. This psalm emerges from the everlasting and uneasy relationship between God and the gods, a relationship that is important for us because it continues in our own time with unabated energy.

"God takes his stand in the council of heaven; he gives judgement in the midst of the gods." We are immediately given the unmistakable message that the gods are very much lesser in this imagined scene.

The rest of the psalm, except for the last verse, is an address from the voice of God. The gods are sternly taken to task. "How long will you ... show favour to the wicked?" God now orders them to do the very things they have not done. "Save the weak and the orphan ... the humble and needy ... the weak and the poor."

By implication the psalmist is describing the attitudes and actions of Israel's God of justice. This particular concept of God will set the religion of Israel apart from that of the surrounding Middle

Eastern world for a long time to come. In contrast with "the gods," the God of Israel is essentially a moral God.

"Now I say to you, 'You are gods ... Nevertheless, you shall die like mortals, and fall." As we noted, this psalm reminds us that the gods are by no means dead. We can agree with this if we understand "the gods" as those enslaving forces that so often demand our ultimate allegiance.

For some, the gods can be political power. For others, it can be possessions; for others, sexual prowess; for yet others, some different egotistical pursuit. The list is long, for the gods are many.

God's words to the gods, " 'You are gods' ... Nevertheless, you shall die" tell us two things. First, the gods—those things that demand our allegiance—are indeed powerful and must not be underestimated. Second, the lesser gods of human choosing eventually fail to satisfy fully the trust and hope invested in them.

At the end of the day we will want to echo the words of the psalmist, "Arise, O God, and rule."

≈

Identify some of the false "gods" currently active in your society. Identify some of the false "gods" currently active in your own life. Ask God to help you and your society to acknowledge these "gods," to evaluate them, and to seek the will of God.

Psalm 83

O God, do not be silent … For your enemies …
take secret counsel against your people.

Within twenty-four hours of the United Nations declaring the existence of the state of Israel in 1948, seven Arab armies attacked the new state. Since then the struggle for survival has become almost mythic in Jewish memory. Reading the psalms makes us realize that everyone involved in this struggle must have had a strong sense of *déjà vu*, particularly if they were versed in their scriptures and knew this psalm.

"They have said, 'Come, let us wipe them out from among the nations.' " Those very words were repeated in 1948. We have merely to exchange an ancient map for a modern one to see that the twentieth-century alliance against Israel was basically the same as the biblical alliance.

"Edom and the Ishmaelites; the Moabites and the Hagarenes" all came from the south. "Gebal, and Ammon, and Amalek" came from the east. "The Philistines" came from the south-east. "Those who dwell in Tyre," the Phoenicians, came from today's south Lebanon. The psalm lists even more enemies, impressing us with the formidable forces that threaten the psalmist's contemporaries.

To build confidence in those who have to meet this forbidding challenge, the psalmist lists former victories. "Midian … Kishon … Endor" are place names where enemies were routed in the past. "Sisera … Oreb … Zeëb" are leaders that were beaten back. They in their time also said, "Let us take for ourselves the fields of God."

In the fashion of a speaker or poet of that day, the psalmist piles up vivid images to describe the anticipated victory over these new enemies. In his mind victory is certain because God is on the side of Israel.

It is not easy for us to use such a psalm for our purposes. The certainty that God is on our side in a national sense is foreign to most people today. We have learned in recent years that people who believe this can perpetrate extraordinarily cruel and violent acts.

The gift of this psalm might be to guide us in thinking of these enemies as the forces that attack the inner citadel of our lives—fear, anxiety, anger, depression, to name a few. As we fight these personal battles, the realization that a loving God is truly on our side can be a profound source of strength.

≈

Ask God to be with you. Consider a difficult feeling that troubles your life. Let yourself feel the feeling. Examine the motives behind the feeling. Be kind but honest with yourself. Ask God to give you the insight, courage, and compassion to respond.

Psalm 84₁

The Lord God is both sun and shield;
he will give grace and glory.

It is about ten o'clock at night in a city hospital. A parishioner who has become an old friend is dying after a long and difficult struggle. Speaking very close to his ear, I quietly begin, "My soul has a desire and longing for the courts of the Lord; my heart and my flesh rejoice in the living God."

As if coming back from a long way off, he opens his eyes, smiles, and says, "The sparrow has found her a house," then closes his eyes again and says nothing more. But he has responded enough to let me know that, at some level of consciousness, he was reciting this psalm with me.

In all scripture there is probably no more lovely expression of the pilgrim journey of human life. The end of pilgrimage for the psalmist is the temple courts, "the courts of the Lord." But for us who share this psalm, the final goal can be elsewhere. For some it will be a familiar place of worship. It will mean finding "a house … by the side of your altars," where one acknowledges, without any argument or holding back, the presence of "my King and my God."

To understand our life in terms of pilgrimage, so that our "hearts are set on the pilgrims' way," is to possess a recipe for happiness. Even though some of the journey will offer no choice about going through a "desolate valley," we are assured that this part of the journey will provide a companion, and that the desolation will not be without "springs" and "pools of water."

As the journey goes on, the pilgrim comes to realize the importance of moving through solitariness and contemplation of the narrow self and its needs. "One day in your courts is better than a thousand in my own room." The pilgrimage through the self leads to the God who is both within and beyond the self.

The pilgrim also learns that it is necessary deliberately to place oneself in the path and presence of God. The spiritual quest must become intentional. It is necessary "to stand at the threshold of the house of my God."

If we can remain open to encounter with God, there will be glimpses of grace. Even though we cannot retain these moments, they will be remembered. "For the Lord God is both sun and shield; he will give grace and glory."

≈

Recall intimations of God experienced in some place of worship. Recall intimations of God experienced in your own soul. Ask God to guide you into the presence of God in the sacred places, both of the world and of your own soul.

Psalm 85

Mercy and truth have met together;
righteousness and peace have kissed each other.

Jürgen Moltmann, a German theologian, reminds us that there are two Latin words for the future—*futurum* and *adventus*. He describes *futurum* as a future that we project, based on trends and extrapolations. He calls it the future of social calculation.

He describes *adventus* as a future that comes toward us from beyond, infinitely open to possibility. He calls it the future of ethical anticipation. We engage *adventus* by asking ourselves what we would like the future to be, then acting in a way that tries to make it so. In this psalm we listen to someone sing of the future as *adventus*.

"Restore us then, O God our Saviour ... Will you be displeased with us for ever? ... Will you not give us life again?" It is obvious that Israel is in trouble. If God were not angry, things would be otherwise. For most people in the Western world today, it is no longer possible to link the state of the world with the anger of God. For the psalmist this was a given.

Something must be said or done to lift the hearts of the people. The psalmist attempts to trigger memories of good times. In the past "you have been gracious to your land, O Lord, you have restored the good fortune of Jacob [meaning all of us as a people]. You have forgiven the iniquity of your people ... You have withdrawn all your fury."

The wish to have good times again kindles the determination

to act in a way that will bring them back. The psalmist feeds a suggestion to the listening minds. "I will listen to what the Lord God is saying, for he is speaking peace to his faithful people."

Having recalled good memories of what was and could be again, the psalmist now takes his listeners into the future. He emphasizes how readily available the grace of God is. "Truly, his salvation is very near to those who fear him." It is within their grasp to begin the process of change that will bring what everyone wishes.

In a magnificent image the psalmist brings to mind a land reconciled and happy. "Mercy and truth have met together; righteousness and peace have kissed each other." The blessing of God will issue in a bright future, assuring "prosperity" and "increase," and again "righteousness" and "peace."

In a complex and even dangerous present, we need to follow the example of the psalmist. In a world torn by human strife, we need to maintain our hope in the possibility of a future where "righteousness and peace have kissed each other."

≈

Consider a situation in the world, and your own life, where strife reigns. Recall a situation in the world, and your own life, where reconciliation and healing reign. Ask God to guide you and to bring reconciliation and healing into all strife.

Psalm 86

Great is your love toward me;
you have delivered me from the nethermost Pit.

There is an immediate sense of someone in the depths of depression. "O Lord ... answer me, for I am poor and in misery."

There is also an alarming scent of fear, its source not yet defined. "Keep watch over my life ... save your servant who puts his trust in you." Later in the psalm we learn the reason for this fear, and it is real and obvious. "A band of violent men seeks my life." The psalmist has good cause to be afraid.

Certain verses in this psalm express two powerful insights. The first insight comes as the psalmist implores God to make possible the kind of relationship between them that can give the psalmist confidence and hope. "Gladden the soul of your servant," he prays. "Give ear, O Lord, to my prayer ... Teach me your way, O Lord ... knit my heart to you that I may fear your name."

The psalmist's reaching out to God suggests a lesson for many of us. Much contemporary spirituality emphasizes the development of self as preparatory to relationship with God. We have almost forgotten that Jewish and Christian faith understands the love of God as constantly reaching toward us, forming us to the degree that we allow ourselves to be formed. Although it is our responsibility to open ourselves to divine love, God is always waiting for us.

The second insight comes as the psalmist experiences the return of a calm and quiet confidence. "Great is your love toward me; you have delivered me from the nethermost Pit." Verses like this occur frequently in the psalms. They can be interpreted as reminiscences of times when everything seemed at low ebb, and when God gave courage and strength to rise again from the depths. But they can also be something more.

The psalms—and other books of the Bible—frequently speak of a hoped-for event as if it has already happened. A prophet in Babylon will imagine God's people having returned to Zion. Already the walls are built, already the houses ring with the voices of children.

Martin Luther King, Jr., used the same device as he "dreamed" a future of peace and harmony. When the psalmist says to God, "You have delivered me from the nethermost Pit," he may be imagining himself as already delivered.

Thinking in this way can become, for any of us, a source of new energy and new resolve.

❧

Consider a difficulty in your life. Imagine God being with you and waiting for you to open yourself to God. Ask God to resolve the situation in a way that is best for all involved. Imagine yourself trusting and resting in the presence of God.

Psalm 87

Glorious things are spoken of you,
O city of our God.

In the city there are taxis and hotels, vendors selling maps and postcards, camels waiting to be ridden. There are also violent explosions, implacable hatreds, crowded streets. Standing on the western slope of the Mount of Olives and looking across the Kidron Valley at the city, one can be mesmerized by the sight. Jerusalem! The name itself holds a kind of power.

"Of Zion it shall be said, 'Everyone was born in her.' " This is true especially for the believer, the person for whom the pages of the Bible have at least some familiarity, even if only from memories of early years. Yet even those without this background can tell you that standing and looking at Jerusalem is to be called and held in a way difficult to define.

It is as if there are two cities inside oneself—the city of one's birth, and this city of hills and dust and golden stone. "I count Egypt and Babylon among those who know me; behold Philistia, Tyre, and Ethiopia." And we can add the names of a thousand other countries before completing the verse and saying again, "in Zion were they born … The Lord will record as he enrolls the peoples, 'These also were born there.' "

The psalmist is recalling the beauty of the temple liturgies. "The singers and the dancers will say, 'All my fresh springs are in you.' " For us this verse can have other meanings, perhaps explaining why this city is indeed home for a believer. Here on these hills much of what has formed us came to be—events that have shaped our faith, manuscripts that have passed that faith on to us, men and women who, from the remote past to the present day, have led and loved and taught us.

To the extent that all these have given us a faith, they have become for us the singers and dancers in our hearts and minds. And if we but realize it, they are the fresh springs that give our lives a sense of joy and meaning.

≈

Recall a person from the remote past who has guided and taught you. Recall a person from your own time who has guided and taught you. Give thanks to God for them. Ask God to bless them. Ask God to let you be an inspiration to others.

Psalm 88

Lord, why have you rejected me?
why have you hidden your face from me?

American law and American concepts of justice will probably take a long time to come to terms with the result of the O. J. Simpson trial. The verdict engendered widespread shock. In spite of much public cynicism about the law, most people assume the efficacy of justice and expect it to be served. In this case, it seemed to have been manifestly not served.

To understand many of the voices in the psalms, we need to appreciate an assumption of the psalmist's world—at the core of what we can know about the nature of God lies justice. It may not be possible on earth to receive this justice today, or even in the near future, but eventually justice must and will be served.

This is what enables the psalmist to cry out as he does. "By day and night I cry to you." His despair knows no bounds; his readiness to express it knows no hesitation. "I am full of trouble ... at the brink of the grave ... like one who has no strength; Lost among the dead."

The psalmist not only seeks assistance from God, but also—in a way that startles and challenges our modern minds—he attributes his miseries to God. "You have laid me in the depths of the Pit ... Your anger weighs upon me heavily ... You have put my friends far from me."

The voice now changes to accusation mingled with sarcasm. "Do you work wonders for the dead? ... Will your loving-kindness

be declared in the grave?" There can be one only reason for what has happened. "Lord, why have you rejected me? … Your blazing anger has swept over me."

The psalmist's understanding of God situates everything that happens in a context of meaning. God is the source of all things and all events—good and bad. But—and this is a crucial factor in the spirituality of the psalmist's world—God is not only the source of all but also the source of justice. And so, the psalmist has every right to demand this justice, and also every reason to expect it.

Thus, in the darkest moments of life is placed the light of hope that makes all the difference.

❧

Ask God to be with you. Consider a difficult situation in your life. Consider a difficult situation in the world. Ask God to give you understanding of both your responsibility and God's justice in the situation. Ask God to let the light of hope shine.

Psalm 89

Righteousness and justice
are the foundations of your throne;
love and truth go before your face.

We are in the company of someone who has experienced a terrible calamity. They can hardly bring themselves to believe it. God has broken a promise that the psalmist's people have always believed was unbreakable.

"I am persuaded that your love is established for ever." There is puzzlement and disbelief in the voice. In spite of God's previous assurance, something has gone terribly wrong. "I will establish your line for ever." So God had said to David and his people.

The psalmist reflects on what Israel has always believed to be true. "The heavens bear witness ... to your faithfulness ... your faithfulness is all around you." He now considers the evidence for his belief. "You rule the raging of the sea ... you have scattered your enemies ... Righteousness and justice are the foundations of your throne ... the Holy One of Israel is our king."

The psalmist continues to wrestle with this impossible puzzle. He spells out the promises categorically made to David the king, the great hero of their history. "My hand will hold him fast," God said. "No enemy shall deceive him, nor any wicked man bring him down ... My faithfulness and love shall be with him ... I will establish his line for ever." The psalmist keeps on repeating these promises of God, as if by saying them often enough he will undo what has happened.

But there comes a moment when the reality hits home. "You have cast off and rejected your anointed ... You have broken your covenant with your servant ... You have exalted the right hand of his foes ... covered him with shame." A flood of bitter recrimination against God pours out. God seems to have betrayed them in spite of a covenant that was supposedly unbreakable.

Now, contrary to all expectation, we hear the very last line of the psalm, and we are astonished. "Blessed be the Lord for evermore! Amen, I say, Amen." In spite of everything that has happened, faith in this God remains unshakeable.

Here in a single line is the gift this psalm has for us. Our own prayer is to possess such a quality of faith, particularly in times when life is shadowed and everything seems under threat.

≈

Consider some intractable problem afflicting your life or the world. For yourself or others, ask God for courage to consider the problem, to discover the truth, and to respond with compassion. Every time you think of it, invite God into the situation.

Psalm 90

So teach us to number our days
that we may apply our hearts to wisdom.

Coming on this psalm is rather like walking around St. Peter's Basilica in Rome and suddenly discovering the power and beauty of *La Pieta*, Michelangelo's incomparable statue of Mary holding her dead son.

The theme of this psalm is not unique. In many other psalms God is approached with awe and humility. God's graciousness is requested. Blessing on God's people or the psalmist is prayed for. All this is familiar.

The difference here is the majesty of the language that the psalmist uses to voice his pleas. The words and themes match one another. "Before the mountains were brought forth, or the land and the earth were born" eloquently captures a sense of almost endless time. "You turn us back to the dust, and say, 'Go back, O child of earth,' " conveys the reality of the human situation without being cruelly dismissive.

A mirror is held up for us, and we see our fragility and transience. "We fade away suddenly like the grass ... we consume away in your displeasure ... Our iniquities you have set before you ... we bring our years to an end like a sigh." The psalmist is not just indulging in romantic melancholy but approaching an invaluable discovery. To realize our transience is to realize the necessity of living with meaning. "So teach us to number our days that we may apply our hearts to wisdom."

It is startling to realize that this magnificent tribute to God does not arise out of the psalmist's well-being or happiness or good fortune. This psalm has been composed during, or soon after, a time of considerable suffering. "Return, O Lord; how long will you tarry?" reminds us of a mysterious and wonderful truth. God communicates with us who seek him, not only when we sense the divine presence around and within us, but even when God seems to be absent.

Even more impressive is the paradoxical, "Make us glad by the measure of the days that you afflicted us and the years in which we suffered adversity." Because of the unbreakable bond between a people and their God, even difficult and demanding times have meaning.

One does not easily leave this psalm without offering a secret prayer that our own bond with God may be as strong and mature.

❧

Recall a difficult time in your life. Consider how you learned and grew in the situation. Recall a difficult time in the life of others. Consider how others learned and grew. Pray for a strengthening and deepening relationship with God, for yourself and others.

Psalm 91

You are my refuge and my stronghold,
my God in whom I put my trust.

Almost two hundred years lie between Thomas Hobbes's bitter observation that "life is ... nasty, brutish, and short," and the bumper sticker informing us that "Life is hard and then you die." Both statements voice the sadness and loneliness of many contemporary people, and both are in utter contrast to the voice of the psalmist.

From a twenty-first century sadness and loneliness disguised by bitter humour, we turn to a quality of confidence that is almost forgotten. The psalmist sees life as lived "in the shelter of the Most High ... the shadow of the Almighty." He knows God as his "refuge" and "stronghold" and describes this relationship in terms of utmost tenderness.

If we are prepared to hear these words addressed to us personally, then we will be assured of deliverance from "the snare of the hunter and ... pestilence." We will "find refuge under his wings." In God we will have "a shield and buckler." We "shall not be afraid" of life's all too present terrors.

We are asked to imagine ourselves surrounded with angels—walking through life with a sense of being guarded and guided. No promise is made that we will live without burdens and troubles. At times we will need, and desperately seek, help. We are assured that, in such times, God "is bound to me in love." We will be delivered, protected, rescued.

The power of this psalm lies in its readiness to speak of our relationship with God in terms of confidence and intimacy. This is nothing less than a relationship between lover and beloved. Our contemporary sensibilities have become almost incapable of accepting such an attitude toward God. Most of us may be able only grudgingly to acknowledge the possibility while entertaining a furtive hope that the possibility might be true.

Yet, far from accommodating itself to our attenuated contemporary trust, the psalm ends with a display of sublime confidence in God. We hear God speaking in the final verses. Referring to the psalmist, and therefore by implication to each one of us, God says,

> [You are] bound to me in love,
> therefore will I deliver [you];
> I will protect [you], because [you know] my name.
> [You] shall call upon me, and I will answer [you].
> I am with [you] in trouble;
> I will rescue [you] and bring [you] to honour.
> With long life will I satisfy [you],
> and show [you] my salvation.

❧

Recall, and perhaps make a list of, the many good things in your life—memories, people, events, possessions. Let yourself experience the feelings associated with these good things. Let yourself feel grateful and friendly toward God for all these things.

Psalm 92

You have made me glad by your acts, O Lord;
I shout for joy ... I am anointed with fresh oil.

To read this psalm can also be to experience the mood of two great songs from the world of musical theatre.

One is from *My Fair Lady*; the other from *South Pacific*. The first is sung by Eliza Doolittle as soon as she is alone after her first successful outing in high society with Henry Higgins. Again and again she sings, "I could have danced all night." The second is sung by Nellie Forbush when she realizes that her relationship with Emile de Beque has become a love affair. She almost leaps on to the stage and sings, "I'm in love, I'm in love, I'm in love with a wonderful guy."

If we can accord the psalmist such a thing as a stage entry, he too seems to leap into our company. "It is a good thing to give thanks to the Lord ... to sing praises ... of your faithfulness." The phrases tumble over each other as if, in his joy, he can't get them out fast enough.

The mood continues. "You have made me glad ... I shout for joy." For once the reality of things, the fact that "the wicked grow like weeds, and all the workers of iniquity flourish" doesn't seem to matter. In his present euphoria everything shrinks in size before the sheer greatness of the Lord. About himself the psalmist is perfectly confident. "The righteous ... Those who are planted in the house of the Lord shall flourish [and] shall still bear fruit in old age."

Such moments come to us all from time to time. We think of

them as "highs." We have come to expect that such moments will not last long, but they can be extremely valuable. They provide an opportunity to escape from the prison of our narrow self, what the psalmist sometimes calls "the Pit." Sometimes a "high" can lift us out of ourselves and enable us to reach into the realm of the heart and soul, where God waits to be discovered and to offer us the riches of life.

There is a moment when the psalmist says, "You have made me glad by your acts, O Lord." We might recall his words in times of well-being and joy. We are often given to dismiss times of unexplained joy as "just" this or that, "just" an adrenalin rush, "just" some chemical change or psychological process. To think of these moments instead as an anointing from God is to see them as a gift given, a blessing received.

Recall a time when you experienced real happiness, elation, or ecstasy. Let yourself enjoy the feeling. Share the feeling with God. Thank God for this feeling. Ask God to let others experience such feeling and to let it bring them closer to God.

Psalm 93

Mightier than the sound of many waters …
mightier is the Lord who dwells on high.

Partly because they were not from a seagoing race, the biblical writers rarely situate us in an ocean setting. But I can't help wondering if this psalm was first uttered beside some body of water. I can recall standing on the shore at Caesarea during a February storm, the white-topped waves lashing the land. I felt like shouting into the wind. I wonder if the psalmist felt the same at this moment.

There is a hint of this feeling in the declamatory way this song begins. "The Lord is king." The words sound a note of defiance, as if the elements of air and water are being challenged to bow their heads before their creator. "The Lord … has put on splendid apparel … girded himself with strength." Very few sights are as majestic as a roaring sea.

Now there is another note of defiance. The chaos of the sea seems to contrast with the solidity of the land, which immediately brings to mind the changelessness and power of God. "Your throne has been established; you are from everlasting."

But then suddenly the psalmist's thoughts are pulled back to the storm. He hastily retreats before a rogue wave that boils around him and threatens to tow him under. His voice gasps out, "The waters have lifted up … their voice … their pounding waves." But once again the power of the elements reminds him of another power, another majesty. "Mightier than the sound of many waters … mightier is the Lord."

Now the psalmist seems to retreat from the shoreline and move toward higher ground, perhaps seeking shelter. Around him is the reassuring sight of solid stone and stout wood. There is a sense of refuge and peace. He can draw breath.

His memory recalls other more magnificent stones, more beautiful wood. His thoughts are in the Lord's house in Jerusalem. From here it is only a short step to the contemplation of God's law, timeless and sure, with its own majesty. "Your testimonies are very sure, and holiness adorns your house, O Lord."

Nature in all its moods is one of the doors opening into the presence of God. Because most of us today live in an urban context, we need to give ourselves opportunity to walk through the door of nature much more often than we do.

≈

Recall or visit a wonderfully inspiring natural scene. Let yourself rest in the scene. Give your senses free play. Let yourself see, hear, and feel the beauty around you. Reach out for God's presence in the scene and in yourself. Give thanks to God.

Psalm 94

If the Lord had not come to my help,
I should soon have dwelt in the land of silence.

To read this psalm is to see newspaper headlines and television images from recent decades. The voice of the psalmist is the voice of countless men and women who have had to live under corrupt and cruel regimes where people feel a terrible sense of helplessness.

"O Lord God of vengeance, O God of vengeance, show yourself." The naming of God as vengeance, and the repeating of that name, is chilling. The vehemence of the speaker screams in one's ear. "Give the arrogant their just deserts." Nothing is so terrible as watching helplessly while evil is perpetrated with absolute impunity by people who relish what they do. "They bluster in their insolence … evildoers are full of boasting. They crush … afflict … murder."

Perhaps most terrible of all is the hubris or pride of those who feel that ultimate power lies in their hands. "They say, 'The Lord does not see.' " The psalmist challenges their assumption of power as the illusion it really is. "When will you fools understand? … The Lord knows our human thoughts; how like a puff of wind they are." We have to assume that the psalmist speaks in private moments and secret places or, if he speaks in public, that he receives contemptuous dismissal from a regime so secure that such words are no threat.

Now the psalmist turns inward, as anyone in such circumstances must do. The situation cannot be changed; therefore, it must be endured. The psalmist's source of inner strength is God. From God comes "rest in evil days," meaning the restfulness that allows strength to be gathered before another ordeal, "until a pit is dug for the wicked."

At this point we hear again the extraordinary degree of trust in God that runs through all the psalms, indeed through the whole Bible. We hear an immense resilience in the cadences of these verses. "The Lord will not abandon his people, nor will he forsake his own. For judgement will again be just."

Now the psalmist begins to draw on personal experience. "As often as I said, 'My foot has slipped,' your love, O Lord, upheld me." Because he trusts in God, he knows that the present situation will eventually reap the whirlwind. "Can a corrupt tribunal have any part with you?" He is utterly confident of the answer. "The Lord our God will destroy them."

❧

Is there now, or has there been in the past, some intractable situation in your life when you have felt helpless and oppressed? Can you discern any good issuing from the situation? Ask God to help all those who suffer from cruelty and oppression.

Psalm 95

Come, let us bow down and bend the knee …
For he is our God,
and we are the people of his pasture.

One has only to be in the Middle East for a short time to realize why water has such an overpowering significance there. Sources of water, the beauty of water, the search for water, hoping for water, fighting over water, praying for water—the episodes are endless, the images vivid, the stories full of conflict.

This psalm is full of the sound of water, sometimes stated directly, sometimes implied. The opening image of God as "the rock of our salvation" comes from the lesson in the long wilderness journey of the Israelites fleeing from Egypt—rocky places were often sources of water. Also "caverns of the earth." At sometime during their journey they emerged from the eastern edge of the Sinai desert to find themselves on the shore of the Red Sea. It was a moment they never forgot. "The sea is his, for he made it."

Now the tone of the psalm changes. The psalmist recalls a wilderness moment around two wells—one bitter and dangerous to drink—when the fragile trust of the people broke down [Exodus 15:23]. There is bitterness in the voice of God. "They put me to the test, though they had seen my works."

The consequence of their lack of trust—years languishing in the brutal terrain of the Sinai—is chilling. "I swore in my wrath, 'They shall not enter into my rest.' " Yet, in spite of all, the link between God and the people holds firm. "We are the people of his pasture and the sheep of his hand."

All the elements in this psalm are true of the situation we find ourselves in as Christians. There is a massive thirst for God, not only in the churches but in society at large. There is a sense that humanity is caught in a wilderness moment between a past wistfully remembered and a future fearfully anticipated. To compound the situation, materialistic science has eroded the certainty that creation is the work of a loving God and that humanity has a covenant with this God.

Yet in the last few years, avant-garde science has been opening frontiers of mystery far beyond previous understanding. And the message of this psalm, plus a major part of scripture, continues to assure us of this mystery. At last, the ancient bond between science and spirituality may be recast, and become again a source of faith and hope.

〰

Find some news of avant-garde science opening new frontiers. Read some scripture describing the greatness of God and creation. Consider the fragility and persistence of life. Ask God to inspire your faith and hope in a universe of love and purpose.

Psalm 96

[God] will judge the world with righteousness
and the peoples with his truth.

There are moments when we are made to realize the vastness of our earth—being alone at sea in a small boat, or in a range of mountain peaks, or in a desert tract of the Middle East. Suddenly we become searingly aware of our finitude, our mortality, our infinitesimal role in the whole scheme of things.

A similar kind of reaction happens when we read this psalm. But now it is not the vastness of the earth that presses on us, but the greatness and majesty of God. "Great is the Lord ... more to be feared than all gods." The domain of this God is "among the nations." This God has formed the world, making it "so firm that it cannot be moved."

This God is also a moral God before whom thought and action are judged. "He will judge the peoples with equity."

This God is the source of all that exists. The psalmist brings each aspect of creation before us and gathers it into a great symphony. "Let the heavens rejoice, and let the earth be glad; let the sea thunder ... let the field be joyful ... the trees of the wood shout for joy." We cannot help recalling those moments in the books of C. S. Lewis and J. R. R. Tolkien, when nature speaks with many voices as in the dawn of creation.

Yet perhaps the greatest tribute that the psalmist gives to God is in the final verses, in three great words that are uttered again and again in the psalms—judgement, righteousness, truth. Beyond even the act of creation itself, these are the highest attributes of God, as the mind of Israel understands divinity. These are the attributes of God that have shaped civilization as we know it.

Yet civilization has shamed these three demands of God, time without number. But the demands never go away. "[God] will judge the world with righteousness and the peoples with his truth."

❧

Ask yourself what the words judgement, righteousness, and truth mean to you. Compare a "worldly" and a "spiritual" understanding of these words. Ask God to guide your thinking and to let divine judgement, righteousness, and truth transform the world.

Psalm 97

Light has sprung up for the righteous,
and joyful gladness for those who are truehearted.

There is much in the psalms to make the environmentalist happy. Again and again we see nature as the domain of God. Seas, mountains, rivers, forests are all sacred. Among them and through them and over them God moves.

As we look at all these images of the presence of God, it is easy to miss something important. Often in the world of environmental concerns, the earth itself is considered sacred. The "Gaia hypothesis" sees the world as a single life form, a living being, coordinating and integrating all the wondrous expressions of created life.

We hear this same wonder in this psalm again and again. The first images are physical and external. "Let the earth rejoice ... the isles be glad. Clouds and darkness are round about ... A fire goes before ... lightnings light up the world ... mountains melt like wax."

But if we merely consider these images, then we betray the psalm. Why does "the earth rejoice"? Because "the Lord is king." God is the source. The clouds and darkness are creatures surrounding God. A fire goes before God. Lightnings proceed from the light of God. Mountains melt in the presence of God. Nature is sacred because it participates in the sacredness of God, the source.

But even so we have not expressed the depths of this and other psalms. Always the psalmist goes beyond and through nature to something deeper and even more significant. Important as it is to see God as creator of nature, it is even more important to probe into the nature of this creating God.

When the psalmist makes these probes, it is always to arrive at the same emphasis. In this psalm we are told that "righteousness and justice are the foundations of [God's] throne." Later we are told that, however wonderful nature and the environment may be, the glory of God is supremely displayed in God's righteousness. The people of God rejoice in the fact that God is a God of justice.

The great gift of this psalm is the conviction in an unshakeable hope. Because God is essentially and eternally just, then justice will eventually triumph no matter how terrible or appalling present circumstances may be.

"Light has sprung up for the righteous," sings the psalmist. A conviction that justice cannot finally be defeated has upheld many of us through dark times.

⁓

Recall or visit some spectacular natural setting. Observe the arrangement of all the various physical features and forms of life. Ask God to let you experience the justice in creation. Pray that God's justice and righteousness may inspire the hearts of all people.

Psalm 98

The Lord has made known his victory;
his righteousness has he openly shown
in the sight of the nations.

One gets the feeling that we have walked in on a huge party. The singing is deafening, the dancers are whirling, arms are waving, food and drink are everywhere. As for any good party, there is a reason—this time a wonderful reason. "The Lord ... has done marvellous things ... won for himself the victory."

But we can't help noticing something peculiar about this victory celebration. Nobody is claiming responsibility for the achievement. We have only to listen to the song to find out why. Everything is ascribed to God.

It is God's right hand and arm that won the victory. The extraordinary thing about this people and their relationship with God is that, if they had experienced defeat instead of victory, they would still have turned to God. The tone would be different. People would be seeking reasons for defeat, but never for a moment would they think of turning away from the God who remains God, no matter what happens.

All events are within the plan and providence of God—defeat or victory, success or failure, good or bad times, rich or lean harvest. All is of God. Therefore, all aspects of life have a reason, and form a part of the vast pattern, known to God alone.

And this is what makes the party possible—the conviction that life possesses meaning and, therefore, inspires hope in the future. "Sing to the Lord with the harp ... and the voice of song. With trumpets and the sound of the horn shout with joy before the King, the Lord." One can't help noticing how human events are somehow linked to the rest of creation, as if the whole universe forms a kind of vast symphony. "Let the sea make a noise and ... the lands ... Let the rivers clap ... the hills ring out."

We come to this party with our tentative and fragmented beliefs. We stand at the edges of the throng, envious of the inner vision that is possible for these people. Yet their inner vision of the ultimacy of God is the great gift that the psalmist and these people offer us. We need only to accept it.

❧

Recall some of your best achievements. Recall some of the best achievements of humanity. Consider what part God played in the working out of these achievements. Give thanks to God for all the good things that you and others have accomplished.

Psalm 99

Proclaim the greatness of the Lord our God
and fall down before his footstool;
he is the Holy One.

Reading this psalm is like walking toward a mountain. At first it stands distant and shining—a shape, no more. A few hours later we can see certain aspects of it—a valley here, an outcrop there. By late afternoon it looms above us, yet it seems more accessible. Its relationship with us has become more intimate. We now see many things previously hidden—the scar from a long ago rock slide, a few streams running down the lower slopes, a small valley piercing deep into the slope.

The psalmist's approach to God resembles our approach to the mountain. Initially he is aware of the infinite distance of God. "The Lord is king ... enthroned ... great in Zion ... high above all peoples." We can only be awed by God's majesty. It is like a mountain peak. It makes us aware of our own pitiable creatureliness. Our very existence seems utterly irrelevant to the divine majesty.

Yet the psalmist brings his description to a climax by defining God as "the Holy One." He seems to be saying that the ultimate greatness is found in holiness. Now, as he approaches the divine mystery, he notices other things about the nature of God. "Lover of justice ... you have executed justice." We are hearing that an essential element in being holy is also being just—not just talking about justice, but also doing justice.

Approaching still nearer to the presence of God, the psalmist sees that he is not alone. He encounters three figures of his own tradition, "Moses and Aaron ... and Samuel." It seems that only people who are larger than life can stand in the presence of God. But very quickly the psalmist cuts these great figures down to size. "You were a God who forgave them, yet punished them for their evil deeds."

The message is clear. We don't have to run from the presence of God. Ordinary fallible sinful humanity is welcome to stand in the divine presence. For this reason we can readily join the psalmist when he invites us to "proclaim the greatness of the Lord."

≈

Recall an occasion when you felt insignificant, inferior, and unworthy. Why did you feel this way? Recall that you are made in the image of God, and that, according to St. Paul, Christ dwells in you. Pray that the divine presence may grow and flower in you.

Psalm 100

Be joyful in the Lord, all you lands …
we are his people and the sheep of his pasture.

a few years ago the media reported that Vincent van Gogh's painting of sunflowers had been sold to a Japanese corporation for forty-two million dollars. I was struck by the mysterious way that an artwork created in one place and time succeeds in speaking to all places and all times. It becomes what we call "a universal."

This same extraordinary process typifies the evolution of Jewish thinking about the nature of God. Beginning with a concept of God that was no different from the ideas of others around them, they came to conceive of God as not only first among the gods, but also the only God. They broke through to the realization that all of reality is one. To use the kind of language we are reaching for today—they realized that all of reality is a single unified "web of being."

This is what the opening lines of this psalm implicitly say. "All you lands" means precisely that—all the earth. The assertion that God "has made us" includes not a single tribe or nation, but all humanity. The claim that "we are his people" reveals a startling vision of the essential unity of the human race, long before Marshall McLuhan talked about our global village, long before Teilhard de Chardin proposed the "hominization" of the globe, long before anyone ever knew about something called the Internet.

It is easy to miss the extraordinary contradiction of all these images with the phrase, "the sheep of his pasture." The psalmist is able to return to this intimate rural image without any sense of inconsistency. We have been considering the whole of humanity and the entire earth. Suddenly we are in a farmyard.

This abrupt change is possible for the psalmist because of the limitless dimensions of his concept of God. We may be talking about the entire earth and the whole of humanity, for that matter we may be considering all of time as the domain of God, but—and herein lies the majesty of the biblical concept of divinity—compared to God, even these vast concepts are no more than a field in which a human might walk and work.

No wonder there is cause to "enter his gates with thanksgiving."

⬭

Consider the miracle of our galaxy and intergalactic space.
Consider the miracle of energy waves and subatomic particles.
Consider the miracle of your daily life, your home, work, and play.
Thank God that you participate in the mind of God.

Psalm 101

I will strive to follow a blameless course;
oh, when will you come to me?

The psalmist is in the mood for making good resolutions. We don't know what has gone before, what has sparked this mood. All we know is that something salutary has happened to release a flood of earnest promises about his future behaviour. We hear a long list of "I will" this, and "I will" that.

"I will sing of mercy and justice ... strive to follow a blameless course ... I will walk with sincerity of heart ... I will set no worthless thing before my eyes." There is a final grand flourish. "I will not know evil." For reasons we cannot know, these are the issues currently occupying the self-reforming psalmist.

Now another voice begins to sound in his mind—the voice of God. We cannot help but wonder whether this voice is the real reason for his guilty feelings. "Those who in secret slander their neighbours I will destroy."

Why does this concern trouble him at the moment? Has he himself indulged in slandering others? "Those who have a haughty look and a proud heart I cannot abide." Has he been harbouring some feelings of moral superiority? "Those who act deceitfully shall not dwell in my house." Has he practised some deceit and this recollection is painful? The list ends with the ugliest word of all—*lies*. "Those who tell lies shall not continue in my sight." We wonder what untruths have been told.

Much is made these days of traditional religion being punitive and guilt-inducing. Well-meaning enlightened minds maintain that such attitudes imagine an old-man-in-the-sky-with-a-white-beard kind of God breathing down our necks. But assuming a moral reference point beyond ourselves gives us a mirror—called God—in which we can see those things in our narrow selves that are neither wonderful nor blameless. The image of God within us reflects the light from this mirror into our souls. Such a mirror—such a God—is a treasure beyond price.

There is a line easily passed over in this psalm. "Oh, when will you come to me?" Why do I long for someone to come to me? Because I am not sufficient in myself. My soul, and every human soul, longs for God.

≈

Have you ever felt inadequate to resist a persistent force or achieve a difficult task? Have you ever felt without help? It is a strength, not a weakness, to know our limitations and ask for help. Ask God to give you inspiration, courage, and support.

Psalm 102

The children of your servants shall continue,
and their offspring shall stand fast in your sight.

To read this psalm is to hear something strange to modern ears,
something that occasions a great deal of thinking and writing these
days. For the psalmist there is obviously a deep relationship between
the well-being of the individual and the well-being of society. For
us, these two entities have become dangerously separated.

The first four lines of the psalm contain the words "me" and
"my" no fewer than six times. In quick succession the psalmist
recalls "my prayer … my cry … my trouble … my days … my
bones." We hear verse after verse of personal complaint. "My days
drift away … My heart is smitten … I am but skin and bones …
I am become like a vulture … I lie awake and groan."

There follows perhaps the most desolate statement that a person
of the psalmist's religion and culture could make. "You [God] have
lifted me up and thrown me away." Nothing could more clearly
present an image of utter desolation than this single line.

But now the psalmist becomes aware of the eternal nature of
God. "You, O Lord, endure for ever." This thought floods through
his mind, carrying him beyond his pain toward the suffering of his
society. We perceive the context in which he stands. His community
is reduced to "very rubble." Around him he can hear "the prayer
of the homeless … the groan of the captive" and the terrible fear
of "those condemned to die."

The outer landscape of his country's suffering reflects the

inner landscape of the psalmist's distress. Considering the combined personal and societal suffering, it would be understandable if the psalmist were to lose all hope.

But once again something happens to take his mind from the terrible vista, and once again it is the vision of God. "The foundations of the earth … shall perish, but you will endure." Even the desolation of his society pales in significance before the unimaginable grandeur and glory of creation, the eternal energy that brings constant change, all set within an indissoluble relationship with humanity.

The psalm addresses us in our anxious time. God endures. Therefore the people of God will endure. The man or woman of God will endure. "The children of your servants shall continue, and their offspring shall stand fast in your sight."

❧

Consider some ways that suffering in your society could affect your life. Consider some ways that contentment in your society could affect your life. Ask God to comfort a suffering person you know. Ask God to nurture compassion in the hearts of all people.

Psalm 103

Bless the Lord, all you works of his …
bless the Lord, O my soul.

There are moments in life when each one of us, whether we know it or not, sings the verses of this psalm—perhaps not all the verses, but at least one of them from time to time.

When we are overcome with a wish to express the sheer joy of being alive: "Bless the Lord, O my soul, and all that is within me, bless his holy name." When we know that we have achieved something not by ourselves alone: "Forget not all his benefits." When we realize that we are free from something that has been sapping our energy for a long time: "He forgives all your sins and heals all your infirmities." When we are given a new lease on life by the passing of some terrifying threat: "He redeems your life from the grave." When we have an experience that is intensely physical, and a sense of life courses through the body. "He satisfies you with good things, and your youth is renewed like an eagle's."

Now, as so often in the psalms, we learn that what is true for a person can be true also in a societal sense. A society that is released from oppression and mistreatment will know the same surge of life experienced by an individual. "The Lord executes righteousness and judgement for all who are oppressed." And as God is merciful to an individual, so there will be mercy for the wrongs a society carries out. "[God] has not dealt with us according to our sins."

There are conditions, however. Mercy for a person or a society is reserved for those "who fear him" and "who keep his covenant and remember his commandments."

From his own life to the life of his people—so goes the thinking of the psalmist. What a far cry from our contemporary tendency to shrink into the realm of the narrow self, to think of the self as essentially alone in the midst of countless other selves. The psalmist offers us the gift of what we might call the recovery of corporate consciousness—the vision of ourselves as part of a living body, certainly composed of other unique selves, but all directed and drawn to a reality beyond ourselves, a reality whom the psalmist calls God.

"The Lord has set his throne in heaven ... do his bidding ... hearken to the voice of his word ... do his will." This for the psalmist is the vision that ultimately ennobles and enriches the individual soul, prompting it to cry, "Bless the Lord, O my soul." May this be so for us.

⪼

We often think of turning to God in times of trouble. Do we think of God at other times—a pesky decision faces us, the daily news excites us, some goodness enters our life? Let yourself turn to God in all life circumstances—ordinary and extraordinary.

Psalm 104

You open your hand, and they are filled with good things.
You hide your face, and they are terrified.

I am about nine years of age. It is Wednesday afternoon choir practice. Outside, through the half-open window, I can see the green of the woods opposite the church. Outside is freedom and play. But suddenly, singing through the verses of this psalm, I am transported to a vast romantic landscape. Our piping soprano voices sing, "There move the ships, and there is that Leviathan, which you have made for the sport of it."

In that distant decade, reading different words from another translation, I would have been captured by the sonorous language of Miles Coverdale, writing to me from the sixteenth century, telling me of "the great and wide sea also, wherein are things creeping innumerable, both small and great beasts. There go the ships, and there is Leviathan, whom thou hast formed to take his pastime therein."

But even though the language differs, the same images would have cascaded into my mind. There is the crash and roar of the ocean, and the heaving of some vast form in the waves just beyond the bow of my imaginary ship.

I am using memory to point out the majesty and grand vision of this psalm. The psalmist thinks in vast landscapes and vistas. "You [God] wrap yourself with light as with a cloak" and "make the clouds your chariot ... the winds your messengers." The psalmist parades before us the whole vast canvas of creation: "the waters

... the mountains ... the springs ... the beasts of the field ... the birds of the air."

This God makes "wine to gladden our hearts," and "bread to strengthen the heart." This God makes the sunrise and, in its golden light, fashions another creature. "Man goes forth to his work ... until the evening." And then, as if this were not enough, this God makes Leviathan to come swimming through the breakers, vast and all the more mysterious by being half hidden in the depths.

But whether one is child or adult, this song gives us a majestic vision of the God of this creation. Vast and wonderful and beautiful though creation be, all it takes is that "you [God] hide your face, and they are terrified," or "[the Lord] looks at the earth and it trembles ... touches the mountains and they smoke."

No wonder the psalmist intends to "sing to the Lord as long as I live."

⤳

Consider the life all around you—running up the stem of a plant, pulsing in the wings of a bird, coursing through the veins of your body, weaving together a small group or a whole society. Ask God to open your soul to the energy, healing, and grace of life.

Psalm 105

He led forth his people with gladness …
That they might keep his statutes.

This psalm would immediately be recognized for what it is by an ancient Celtic Druid, a native Indian shaman, an Inuit elder, or those in a thousand cultures whose duty it was, and still is, to retain the history of their people in the form of narrative. This psalm is a song about a single unified people. Yet it is also much more.

First the patriarchs walk the stage. We learn of "the covenant [God] made with Abraham." We catch a glimpse of an early people "few in number, of little account … sojourners in the land." We hear the thrilling story of Joseph, the exile, also "of little account … a sojourner" who becomes powerful. We watch the people multiply until they threaten an empire and are enslaved. We hear Moses and Aaron utter a call to hard-won freedom. The storyteller describes with relish the plagues that afflict their enemies. "Their land was overrun by frogs, in the very chambers of their kings."

Now the people know the wonder and joy of freedom achieved. "In all their tribes there was not one that stumbled." They have "cloud for a covering … fire to give light … quails … bread from heaven." Savagely and unrepentant, however, "they took the fruit of others' toil."

So much for the story, or rather, a chapter in the story of this people. But the psalmist, as always, never omits the One who moves throughout the story—the God who is not only in the story but is also the author of the story. Statements always begin with "the

Lord." It is not a case of "the waters turned into blood" or "Moses came." It is always "the Lord" who does these things. All verbs flow from God. It is God who "works ... speaks ... leads ... hurls ... sends ... strikes down ... opens ... remembers."

The authorship of God could be the missing factor—the all-important missing factor—in the story of our life as a people. When we tell the story of the journey of our people through recent history, from whom do the verbs flow? Alas, usually from ourselves.

It is salutary to look at the last words of this psalm. "He gave his people the lands of the nations ... that they might keep his statutes and observe his laws."

❧

Recall some major events in the "story" of your people. Recall the major events in the "story" of your life. Ask yourself in what ways God participated in these stories. Ask God to increase your perception and enlarge your understanding of the grace of God.

Psalm 106

[God] gave them what they asked,
but sent leanness into their soul.

Many voices echo through the years from my childhood in Ireland. They tell me of different peoples who came again and again from the sea, of battles fought for the island, of Druids who told the stories, of Patricius, the "noble one," who came with a new story of death and resurrection.

Because of these voices I recognize this psalm as a story of the people of God. They have sprung the trap and escaped from Egypt. Now their mettle will be tested. Their first prayer is not that they may have power but, instead, that they may be a just people. "Happy are those who act with justice." If only we could make this our prayer when we tell our own story as a people!

The psalmist recounts the story of Israel with refreshing candour. One verse reveals the human condition with burning sharpness. "He gave them what they asked, but sent leanness into their soul." From now on the song is unrelentingly dark. "They envied … made a bull-calf … worshipped a molten image … forgot God their saviour … refused the pleasant land … would not listen to the voice of the Lord."

This would have been enough, but the storyteller forces us to hear more. "They grumbled … embittered [Moses'] spirit … intermingled with the heathen … worshipped their idols … sacrificed their sons and their daughters to evil spirits … shed innocent blood … were polluted by their actions."

Then come the consequences. "The wrath of the Lord was kindled … those who hated them ruled over them … they were humbled." At this moment everything changes. The hinge word, "nevertheless," takes us from despair to hope, from shame to self-respect. "Nevertheless, [God] saw their distress … remembered his covenant … caused them to be pitied."

Are we prepared to be as honest as the psalmist in telling our own history? Are we capable of self-criticism, facing the shadow side of who we are as a people? Does this psalm sing what we need to hear but perhaps do not wish to?

Unless we decide to face ourselves in this way, we may not be able to pass from captivity to freedom, from despair to hope.

❧

Recall some of the dark episodes in the "story" of your people. Recall some of the dark episodes in the "story" of your life. Ask God to give you strength to face the past with honesty and compassion. Ask God to give divine grace and healing for past wounds.

Psalm 107

Let them give thanks to the Lord for his mercy
and the wonders he does for his children.

In modern action movies there is a sequence in which the hero
or heroine suffers greatly. He or she will be on the verge of being
overcome; in fact, for a short time it will seem as if all is lost. But
the hero emerges triumphant, and we emerge into the real world,
secure in the conviction that, even though reality may often be
otherwise, there is at least the possibility of rescue.

The psalmist would understand such sequences very well, be-
cause he himself writes such scripts, and this psalm is one. In our
case, individualistic as we are, we write about solitary heroic figures
battling external evils. The psalmist, being much wiser, writes of a
people. "All those whom the Lord has redeemed ... [and] gathered
them out of the lands."

Again, being wise, the psalmist writes of this people wrestling
not merely with external enemies, but with the sometimes much
more troublesome enemies within their own minds and hearts.
"They were hungry and thirsty; their spirits languished within them
... Some sat in darkness and deep gloom ... Some were fools and
took to rebellious ways."

The psalmist offers different scenarios from different chapters
in the story of his people. In an ocean storm some of them "reeled
and staggered like drunkards," but God "stilled the storm to a
whisper." For others at another time God "changed rivers into
deserts," and as they wrestled with this, God once again "changed

deserts into pools of water … [God] blessed them, so that they increased greatly."

Throughout his story, the psalmist repeats an admonishing chorus. "Let them give thanks to the Lord for his mercy and the wonders he does for his children." And he ends the psalm with some advice. "Whoever is wise will ponder these things."

Ponder what? Perhaps that the theme of this psalm runs all through scripture! It tells us that the providence of God is finally benevolent, and that therefore the future is essentially hopeful. In our time we do not find this easy to believe. There are many reasons for being pessimistic. A prime reason is that many have forgotten this biblical theme.

For us to forget this theme as a people would be, at best, unwise and, at worst, disastrous.

≈

How would you describe the difference between physical reality and spiritual reality? You may want to use your imagination! Ask yourself which reality would be most likely to endure. Ask God to give you confidence and hope in the reality of the spirit.

Psalm 108

Grant us your help against the enemy,
for vain is the help of man.

I recall an evening in a pub in County Carlow in Ireland when the talk stilled in response to singing by a particularly lovely voice in an adjoining room. When the song ended, someone said that Irish music knows only two moods—the jig and the lament.

This psalm reminds me of that event because, in the world of the psalmist, there is no middle ground. We are either exulting in euphoric praise of God or groaning in abject dejection, either dancing with wild abandon or cringing with despair or guilt.

The beginning of the psalm is deceptive. Our immediate impression is of someone happily greeting a new day, determined to "make melody ... [and] waken the dawn." Coupled with this mood is a confession of untroubled faith in God, whose "loving-kindness is greater than the heavens."

Suddenly we become aware of something previously hidden. There is a sharp change of direction. We discover that, far from enjoying undiluted well-being, with steadfast faith in God, the psalmist is trying to shore up his spirit. Because of a recent experience, he is feeling anything but confident.

"Have you not cast us off ... you no longer go out, O God, with our armies." Now we know that there has been a military setback, perhaps even a defeat. Perhaps the most revealing moment in the psalm is the plea for "help against the enemy." It is interesting that, after this plea for help, we return to a renewed profession of utter trust in God. "With God we will do valiant deeds."

Once again we are receiving a great gift of Hebrew spirituality—the insight that professing trust in God can help to realize what is hoped for. To profess confidence in God, even though our profession may arise from an actual lack of faith, even a felt absence of God, can sometimes result in a burst of the very confidence needed in the moment.

We are being taught by the psalmist to trust—come what may—that God as a transcendent reality is involved in our daily lives. To have such trust is to possess a strong resource for living, helping us at times to believe that "[God's] faithfulness reaches to the clouds."

❧

Have you noticed that confidence in yourself opens you to release personal energy to pursue achievement? Ask yourself whether confidence in God might open you to receive divine energy. Ask God to strengthen your trust and confidence in God.

Psalm 109

They speak to me with a lying tongue …
They repay evil for good.

There is a scene repeated over and over again in old—and not so old—movies. The hero is under attack. He stands alone and defiant. The cause he champions is utterly right. The intent of the enemy is totally evil. Our hero hopes that something known vaguely as "the cavalry" will come to the rescue.

This scenario from popular culture can be found in many psalms. This psalm presents the classic dichotomy. The psalmist plays the hero. His various detractors, critics, and enemies are cast as scoundrels. The hoped-for source of help is God.

In the face of attack the psalmist curses his enemies roundly—not only the enemy, but his whole family. "Let his days be few … Let his children be fatherless, and his wife become a widow." The curses continue to flow, imprecating both parents and descendents.

Suddenly the psalmist ceases his invective and presents himself as the victim. He is "poor and needy." His "heart is wounded." He has "faded away like a shadow." His "knees are weak … [his] flesh is wasted." He concludes his woeful litany by throwing himself on the mercy of God.

How should a contemporary reader respond to all this? At one level there is something decidedly unattractive, even unhealthy, about the psalmist's venting. He projects his negativity outward on to others. In himself he perceives no fault. The psalmist alone seems innocent, faithful, and pure. His approach raises a question about our own faults and our projecting them on to others.

The difference between most of us and the psalmist is that we find it difficult to admit the same level of intensity in our feelings. We would be wise to face the truth of our emotions—our dislikes, even our hatreds. We could express them harmlessly by putting them into words in the privacy of our own thoughts and journals.

This way we might discover how we really feel about someone who deeply dislikes or threatens us, someone who is a rival, an antagonist, or even an enemy. And if we are truly honest with ourselves, we might discover to what extent we harbour those same feelings and direct them toward others.

Having done this, we might acknowledge our helplessness to change others. We can change only ourselves, but we need help. For this, we can place our situation entirely in the hands of God. Responding in this way would be allowing this psalm to speak to us.

❧

Consider someone who appears to think and act negatively toward you. How do you feel about this? To what extent do you harbour negative feelings toward others? Be gentle but honest with yourself. Ask God to give you courage and grace to grow.

Psalm 110

The Lord said to my lord, "Sit at my right hand,
until I make your enemies your footstool."

At the height of the Roman Empire it was the custom to welcome home a particularly successful general with a public procession through the city. He would be given impressive armour, a splendid chariot, and magnificent horses—all to accord him every possible honour. But standing immediately behind him in the chariot would be a slave who had the single duty of repeatedly reminding the general, "Tu es mortalus." You are mortal.

We hear an echo of that custom in this psalm. Obviously, this song is addressed to a king, probably newly crowned. The song is adulatory. It predicts victories to come. "I make your enemies your footstool." It predicts empire building beyond national boundaries by promising to "send the sceptre of your power out of Zion."

We next hear some diplomatic flattery of a person who holds power. The new king is assured that he has been "princely ... from the day of [his] birth." His nativity is described in the most lyrical terms. He was begotten "in the beauty of holiness ... like dew from the womb of the morning."

But this psalm is much more than praise for a powerful ruler. Consider the opening words: "The Lord said to my lord." The first word, "Lord," refers to God, the second "lord" refers to the newly crowned king. From this opening we perceive a salutary order of precedence—all aspects of the future depend on God. "The Lord will send ... The Lord has sworn ... The Lord who is at your right hand."

If there is to be an empire, the Lord will establish it. If enemies are to become footstools, the Lord, not just the king, will bring it to pass. If the king is to become priest, the Lord will make him so. God "will rule over the nations."

The psalmist paints a portrait of a ruler who, in spite of holding every human power, is still the servant of a greater master. Here is the foundation for healthy governance.

✎

Consider a person who rules a nation, an institution, a business, or a household. Consider a desire that rules your heart. How would life be different if you and others regarded God as ruler of all rulers? Pray that God may rule in the hearts of all people.

Psalm 111

Great are the deeds of the Lord ...
and his righteousness endures for ever.

The great mind of Emmanuel Kant gave us the assurance that, although our human knowledge can be no more than perceptions of the truth, we can always think of two things as the ground of reality. He expressed this in a lovely phrase: "the starry heaven above me and the moral law within me." He may have been echoing the beautiful last lines of Dante's *Divine Comedy:* "The love that rules my heart and mind is the love that moves the sun and stars."

It is possible that both these great minds, and many more, are indebted to the psalmist for such insights. All through the psalms the reality of God is presented as the ground of all else. This psalm, a glorious hymn to God, is a fine example. "Great are the deeds of the Lord," says the psalmist. Nothing is more worthwhile as a focus of our study. The defining marks of God are "majesty ... splendour ... righteousness."

Then, as always in the psalms, there is a contrasting theme. Having been honoured in terms of power, God is now praised in terms of gentleness. "The Lord is gracious and full of compassion." This creator of galaxies also "gives food to those who fear him." The main attributes of this God are "faithfulness and justice." In all of this, the psalmist implies that these same attributes should be evident in our humanity.

Through these two themes runs a third. We hear it in phrases such as "his righteousness endures for ever" and "he is ever mindful" and "his commandments are sure." We are given assurance that God is no transient reality. This God can be depended upon through the ages. The truths of this God "stand fast for ever and ever."

Before this God there is only one response possible for the psalmist. God is "holy and awesome." To know this and to act accordingly, to base our lives on such a holy and awesome reality is, for anyone who so chooses, "the beginning of wisdom."

꒰꒱

Consider the vast "external" creation—galaxies, suns, and planets in the universe. Consider the deep "internal" creation—thoughts, emotions, and instincts in the soul. May the vastness and nearness of God amaze and solace your mind and heart.

Psalm 112

Light shines in the darkness for the upright;
the righteous are merciful and full of compassion.

Like clothes, words become threadbare. They cease to be what they once were. For us the word "righteous" and its noun "righteousness" are such words. They are still current in the world of religion, but in the secular world we might say they have gone sour. We would not like to be called "righteous" in the office or at the golf club. To put it mildly, we would not feel praised.

This psalm helps to recapture the true worth of these words and to define what is meant by the words, "they who fear the Lord." This is the primary characteristic of a righteous person—to fear God, not to be afraid of God, but to regard God with reverence, to look to God as the ultimate reference point for our lives.

"Wealth and riches will be in their house." Psalm verses such as this have given rise to a belief among some Christians that wealth is necessarily a proof of being right with God, or righteous. Many Christians would deeply question such an assumption. We might prefer to think that a better test of rightness with God would be the way a person uses his or her wealth.

"Light shines in the darkness for the upright." There is no doubt that having a firm faith in God allows us to look deeply into the dark moments of life and to discern meaning that others may not be able to see. People with such faith "will never be shaken," says the psalmist. Even he might admit, if pressed, that "never" is a big word. All of us at some time in life are shaken to the depth of our souls.

"They will not be afraid of any evil rumours; their heart is right." The last four words form a lovely phrase. But what does it mean that our "heart is right"? If it means "not to be afraid," then for the psalmist, at least one element of being righteous is living trustingly rather than fearfully.

Before he ends his song, the psalmist lists other aspects of being righteous. We are called to be "merciful and full of compassion … to manage [our] affairs with justice … [to give] freely to the poor." Compassionate, just, generous. What a magnificent summing up of the best of human living!

❧

What might be the connection between having "reverence for God" and being "compassionate, just, generous"? Between having "delight" in God's "commandments" and never being "shaken"? How would you nurture such reverence and delight?

Psalm 113

Who is like the Lord our God, who sits enthroned on high
... and lifts up the poor from the ashes.

Among the world's great shrines is the Wailing Wall in the old city
of Jerusalem. Not a moment goes by without somebody standing
before it, head bowed in prayer, body swaying with intensity of feel-
ing. Into the cracks between the massive stones go countless scraps
of paper bearing prayers for every conceivable human need.

There are days when yet another terrible incident has taken
place, another explosion, another massacre, and the wall receives
a throng of people. It looms over them, absorbing their grief and
rage and hope. At such times its name, the Wailing Wall, seems
absolutely appropriate. Yet there are other times when things are
different at the wall, when families celebrate bar mitzvahs and the
atmosphere is more in accord with this psalm.

We hear shouts of acclamation. "Hallelujah! Give praise ...
Let the name of the Lord be blessed." For a moment these verses
seem to lift the pall that lies over so many of the psalms. There
is no threat from enemies, nobody has wronged anyone, nobody
is hurling insults. Instead, there is a prolonged outburst of joy, a
celebration of the being of God.

We get the impression that there is more to this praise than to
the acts of worship we know in much Western Christianity—meas-
ured, rehearsed, and lasting little more than the statutory hour! Here
we see people caught up in celebration that goes on and on, perhaps
even literally "from the rising of the sun to its going down."

Yet one thing remains at the heart of all this joy and celebration. The psalmist's description aptly reflects the way his people understand their God. The Lord may be "high above all nations, and his glory above the heavens," but this same God "takes up the weak out of the dust and lifts up the poor from the ashes." Even further, this God "sets [the poor] with the princes of his people."

Most paradoxical of all, this God, while possessing a "glory above the heavens" and turning the social order upside down by lifting "the poor from the ashes," also has time to consider the sad longing of a human household for the gift of a child.

This psalm offers one of those revealing moments when we understand why Judaism's portrait of God is so all embracing.

≈

We are accustomed to praising God in communal worship celebrations. What are some other times when you might praise God? What are some other ways that you might praise God? Ask God to help you identify times and ways to give thanks and praise.

Psalm 114

What ailed you, O sea, that you fled? …
Tremble, O earth, at the presence of the Lord.

As a twelve-year-old in 1940, I can recall the anxiety as the dramatic rescue of the British army played itself out on the beaches at Dunkirk. I can also remember the relief and joy when the famous fleet of little ships rescued the vast majority of the troops and brought them home to England.

This psalm presents us with the same kind of memories. It begins by recalling the moment "when Israel came out of Egypt." After a long and terrible journey, they find a country. The psalmist looks back on events that have achieved mythical expression in the traditions of his people.

"The sea beheld it and fled," recalls an early moment in their escape from Egypt when, caught between potential death by a pursuing army and death in the sea, they commit themselves in faith to the water. And they cross safely.

"Jordan turned and went back," tells how, in their advance on the city of Jericho, they again enter and commit themselves to water, this time the river Jordan. And again they cross safely. "The mountains … skipped like rams," may suggest tremors in the earthquake-prone area beneath the land they occupied. Or it may present a vivid image of their excitement and joy at a hard-won victory.

The psalmist now asks a series of questions and replies to them. In doing so, he highlights a gulf in thinking between his world and ours. "What ailed you, O sea, that you fled? O Jordan, that you turned back? You mountains, that you skipped like rams?" These are his questions. Here is his reply. "Tremble, O earth, at the presence of the Lord." The psalmist regards all these natural events as the direct result of God's acting in time and history.

We are in a mysterious realm. The contemporary mind has great difficulty linking God directly with human history. Yet it is impossible to deny that, when an event occurs involving our deepest loyalties and relationships—when a loved one recovers from some dreadful illness, or our country emerges from some awful peril—we cannot help but search for a source to which, or to whom, we can offer our thanks.

Millions of adults, in my long-ago twelve-year-old world, offered thanks after the agony of Dunkirk had passed. The psalmist offered thanks in gratitude for a homeland achieved against many odds. In our personal lives, when the "hard rock" of suffering or misfortune is turned into a "flowing spring" of recovery and new life, here too we seek a source for our gratitude.

❧

Recall a time in history when people were saved from disaster. Recall a time when you were saved from disaster. Give thanks to God. Pray that all people may seek God in their suffering, may receive support and relief, and may discover a spirit of gratitude.

Psalm 115

Why should the heathen say,
"Where then is their God?"
Our God is in heaven.

There was a famous incident associated with the terrible siege of Jerusalem and its temple by the Roman army in the year AD 70. The fighting was over. The battered city and temple precincts were occupied by the enemy. Titus, son of the recently crowned Emperor Vespasian—who by now had conquered a succession of peoples and their various gods—had given orders that none other than himself could enter the ruined Holy of Holies in the temple.

Walking in front of his legions, Titus enters. At first, there is silence. Then his troops hear their commander's derisive laughter. Soon the word spreads. There is nothing in the Holy of Holies! One more pathetic religious illusion has fallen to the relentless power and organization of Rome.

How very different the truth was. The Roman mind could not penetrate the depth of Judaism's insights about God. Even as the Roman legion plundered Jerusalem, some Jewish poet may have been singing this very psalm. We listen to his voice. "Why should the heathen say, 'Where then is their God?' Our God is in heaven." This statement certainly does not imagine a God infinitely remote from the human situation. It suggests, rather, that the essence of God lies beyond human perception.

There follows a contemptuous dismissal of the kind of deity the Roman general was expecting to see enshrined in the Holy of

Holies—a statue of bronze, stone, wood, iron, or marble. "Their idols are silver and gold, the work of human hands." The psalmist's disdain extends to those who worship such idols, "Those who make them are like them, and so are all who put their trust in them."

Now we hear a hymn to Israel's Lord, sung in direct contrast to the earlier dismissal of pathetic idols. God's ceaseless activity is compared to an idol's inability to act. The song climaxes with a description of God as nothing less than "maker of heaven and earth."

We are being reminded of the ultimacy of God. For Judaism, God is never an object among other objects, never an element in creation, never definable, in the last resort not even nameable. "God," said Paul Tillich in the last century, "is the ground of all being."

Language falls short, and always will, but Tillich's attempt at a description has been helpful to many.

❧

Do you have some idea of what God must be like? Spend time in quiet meditation considering the qualities that you would expect to find in God. Ask a trusted friend to share their idea of God with you. Ask God to enlighten your mind and heart.

Psalm 116

How shall I repay the Lord
for all the good things he has done for me?

Recently, on answering the phone, I heard the voice of a friend who for weeks had been facing the possibility that medical tests might discover a brain tumour. Just before phoning he had received news that the tests were negative, that his condition was benign and could be treated. I have never heard so clearly the human response to the lifting of a terrible burden.

To read this psalm is to meet such a response. "The cords of death entangled me; the grip of the grave took hold of me; I came to grief and sorrow." We hear the appeal that is sometimes an agonized whisper, sometimes a cry, sometimes a scream. "O Lord, I pray you, save my life."

The memory of terror just experienced releases a flood of renewed gratitude to God. The psalmist rushes from a paralyzing fear to a wild, almost manic, thankfulness. God is "gracious ... full of compassion ... watches over the innocent." God has "helped me ... treated [my soul] well ... rescued my life."

Then, in a way most of us know from experience, the recollection of terror stabs home again. "In my distress I said, 'No one can be trusted.' " There is another rush of intense relief and a series of impassioned resolutions. The psalmist promises to "lift up the cup of salvation and call upon the name of the Lord." From now on he will "fulfill my vows ... in the presence of all [God's] people." This promise is made twice in an effusion of good intentions.

We can imagine the psalmist reiterating promises until he dances out of sight, seeking others to tell of his good fortune. To speak of the psalmist in this way is not in any sense to sneer at his expression of immense relief after a terrible experience.

In the case of my friend, it was the threat of serious illness. It can be many things. The interminable wait for a potentially damaging legal verdict. The helpless feeling that we have lost the love of someone we care for very much, only to discover that all is well and the future beckons. The fear of not knowing whether a business venture will succeed, when everything we possess has been risked on the outcome.

The day comes when we know we have turned a corner. All will be well. Each of these situations is the stuff this psalm is made of. It is one of those passages of scripture that makes us realize how well the Bible knows our human nature.

❧

Ask yourself the question posed by the verse beginning this reflection. Consider how you might "repay" God by nurturing an awareness of God's gifts to the world, others, and yourself. May we respond with grateful hearts to the abundance of God's grace.

Psalm 117

Praise the Lord, all you nations …
For his loving-kindness toward us is great.

With one exception, this is the shortest of all the psalms. Hardly has it time to become a song before it ends! It gives us a concentrated exclamation of praise.

This psalm is like those shouts we hear in support of a school or university game. They are short, passionate, full of energy! Our feelings explode in a burst of enthusiasm. But we can't sustain it. We need to draw breath and get ready for the next threat to our goal or the next goal scored.

But, of course, this shout is not about football, hockey, or basketball. It's about God, and this makes it infinitely more significant. If we have to express something very important to us, but we know we have only a few moments, then we think very carefully about how we use the time. These few lines are extremely interesting. Presumably they express what the psalmist and his people wished more than anything else to say about God.

"Praise the Lord, all you nations." A moment's thought will impress us with the immense claim implicit in this admonition. Here is a tiny nation, often surrounded by great empires—at times invaded by them—asserting that its God is also the God who rules these same empires.

"His loving-kindness toward us is great." Again the implicit claim is of vast significance. The whole of humanity is being assured of the essential benevolence of providence. This God above the gods is a good God. "The faithfulness of the Lord endures for ever." This God may be trusted. This God is not capricious, as are other gods. A contemporary Jewish voice has reiterated this conviction. "God" said Albert Einstein, "does not play dice with the universe."

This short psalm encapsulates in a few words the deepest affirmations we can make about the human situation. We exist within a creation that possesses an essential meaning and purpose. This meaning and purpose may be hidden from us but exists within the mind or being of God. This purpose and meaning is finally for our good.

A huge assumption? Most certainly. Yet it is the basis of all human creativity and hope.

≈

The "purpose and meaning" of human life "is finally for our good." How would you describe this "good"? Consider some of the sayings and "kingdom" parables of Jesus in answer to this question. Ask God to deepen your insight into the mystery of life.

Psalm 118

You are my God, and I will thank you;
you are my God, and I will exalt you.

Perhaps I am over-dramatizing, but I cannot read the opening
verses of this psalm without seeing a sweating bloodied warrior
leaping to a promontory above a victorious army and shouting,
"Give thanks to the Lord, for he is good," and the whole army
responding, "His mercy endures for ever."

Again the solitary figure shouts, "Let Israel now proclaim."
Again a few thousand voices respond, "His mercy endures for
ever." For a third time the warrior exclaims, "Let those who fear
the Lord now proclaim," and the battlefield rings with, "His mercy
endures for ever."

Later in the psalm we again hear the army shouting as one
man, spears lifted at each cry, "The right hand of the Lord has
triumphed! the right hand of the Lord is exalted! the right hand
of the Lord has triumphed!"

As in a movie, when a camera scans from a panoramic scene
to a single individual, we now become aware of one person, the
psalmist. He may be reflecting about the fear and horror of battle.
He remembers the feeling of being trapped. "They hem me in, they
hem me in on every side … They swarm about me like bees … like
a fire of thorns." Then he recalls the sense of being helped from
beyond himself, of possessing a resource he can trust. "I was pressed
so hard that I almost fell, but the Lord came to my help."

Woven through this psalm is the impression of having endured an extremely testing time and having come through safely, even triumphantly. This is true of Israel as a whole, at least its army; but it is realized also by an individual, the psalmist.

This psalm provides a salutary reminder to us who live in a more individualistic age than the psalmist. By weaving together individual experience and communal experience, individual ordeal and communal ordeal, individual survival and communal survival, the psalmist reminds us of the links between the issues of our personal lives and those of our community and nation. One is inextricably bound up with the other.

As John Donne remarked long ago, "No man is an island." Good counsel for all of us to hear!

❧

Without your community or nation, what necessities of life would you lack? What pleasures of life would you lack? Because of you, what necessities and pleasures do your community and nation enjoy? Thank God for the gift of sharing with others.

psalm 119

I will meditate on your commandments
and give attention to your ways.

Just as the works of Shakespeare comprise a collection of individual sonnets, so the psalms include this long psalm that is really a collection of short psalms on a single theme. The collection is significant for us is because it flies in the face of an assumption made by many in today's society.

The entire psalm is an extended meditation on the existence of the law of God. The psalmist calls this law by many names. At various times it is God's word, God's judgements, God's commandments, God's statutes, God's decrees. Contemporary culture doubts the existence of a body of truth beyond our own thoughts, perceptions, tastes, or opinions. Because of this, Christian faith—indeed all religious faith—is already clashing head on with the culture we live in.

This collection of psalms also clashes with the way many today see themselves as "victim." The psalmist is constantly pointing us away from this view. He encourages us to respond to life, to act, and to take initiatives. "Happy are they ... who walk in the law of the Lord ... and seek him."

To live like this, we know we need God's grace. "With my whole heart I seek you." Having sought divine grace and acted, we then accept responsibility for our decisions and actions. Life is seen as a dialogue of belief and action between God and the believer. "You laid down your commandments, that we should fully keep them."

The world of the psalms is intimately linked with God, but the psalmist never considers human beings as merely passive receivers of divine directions. He sees us as called to constant decision and initiative. The psalm is alive with active verbs preceded by a firm and unapologetic first-person singular. "I will thank you ... I will keep your statutes ... I seek you ... I treasure your promise ... I will meditate on your commandments ... I will not forget your word."

The psalmist is under no illusions about where in human life responsibility lies. Life proceeds from our "acting" rather than "being acted on." There is no role of victim here. There is, instead, a certainty that truth exists, and that our life's vocation is to search it out.

When we sing any section of this great sustained work, we encounter a song that challenges our culture to acknowledge the reality of God's law, before which we are accountable and from which we draw inspiration.

❧

Do you find yourself in a situation where you feel a victim? Could you possibly take responsibility for your situation? Ask God to help you to analyze the situation, to honestly discern your weaknesses and strengths, and to show you a way forward.

Psalm 120

Too long have I had to live
among the enemies of peace.

It can be fascinating to search for those tiny clues in a piece of writing that give us information about the writer. There is something in this short psalm that suggests a certain solitariness.

The mood is melancholy. We get the impression that not many friends are around at the moment, or if they are, the writer is not open to their friendly approaches. There is a hint that something unpleasant has been experienced. "When I was in trouble." But whatever it was, he has come through it. "I called to the Lord, and he answered me."

It is intriguing to guess at the trouble. We might start with the place names. They are very far apart. Meshech is in southern Asia Minor, or today's Turkey, and Kedar is in the general area of northern Saudi Arabia. Obviously, the psalmist has had to live in these places—and perhaps others—for a considerable time. He has had no choice about this: "I must lodge."

By the time we encounter the psalmist, his surroundings have actually become "hateful." There is an intensity in the way he says this. The places where he finds himself are not merely distasteful or unpleasant. They are hateful!

We may not be far wrong if we decide that the psalmist is a trader. The "lying lips" and "deceitful tongue" he has had to experience may be those of crafty competitors. He is seething at the level of deceit around him. Obviously, "hot glowing coals" are too good for these tongues!

At this stage, just as he ends his emotional tirade, the psalmist's real agenda appears. Since these people are enemies anyway, what else would he expect? He comes as a peaceful traveller. They think of nothing but war. How then can such people be other than deceitful?

This song comes to us from across the centuries but sings a timeless truth. Alienation from our circumstances colours all our dealings. We lose any capacity to trust. Competitors become enemies. Surroundings—workplace, colleagues, staff meetings—become hateful. It seems that no further good can be found in the situation.

Yet we need to look again at the way that this long-ago beleaguered figure continually has the name of his Lord on his lips. Twice he speaks of calling on the Lord. Again he asks the Lord to deliver him. Whatever circumstances we are in, personal or professional, it can make all the difference to have a sense that we live—even if life is sometimes a struggle—in the presence, and with the grace, of God.

※

Consider a situation that causes, or has caused, you to feel oppressed by difficult people or circumstances. Now ask God to let you feel the divine presence around you. Let your life flow into the life of God, and let the grace of God flow into your life.

Psalm 121

My help comes from the Lord,
the maker of heaven and earth.

Sometimes when we hike a trail or drive a highway, we happen upon some wonderful vista that takes our breath away. So it is now, as we discover again this exquisite poem.

To identify with the psalmist we must stand on the Mount of Olives and look down into the valley where the tiny city of David once clung to a lower ridge. We realize how vulnerable that fortress was to enemies who might at any time appear on the higher escarpments around it. To "lift up my eyes to the hills" from a street of that city, and to see enemy fighters poised above, would be to feel an urgent need for help.

In that long-ago fortress even the best sentry was human and, therefore, could fall asleep. It would have been essential for a citizen to feel guarded and cared for by one who needs "neither slumber nor sleep." For the psalmist this guardian is the Lord who "watches over you," who is "your shade at your right hand."

There is a lovely insight easily missed in the image of the Lord as our "shade." Rich and powerful people usually had a servant stand beside them with an umbrella of palm fronds or some other material to protect them from the brutal sunlight and heat. This line in the poem shares the beautiful idea of God as servant, a beauty we will see manifested centuries later in the person of our Lord Jesus Christ.

So we have a song of unapologetic dependence on God, which

admits that we cannot handle life on our own and need not be ashamed to say, "My help comes from the Lord." Today we find this attitude toward God difficult to sustain. We are still vulnerable to Sigmund Freud's dismissal of faith as childish dependence and projection. Yet most of us have encountered such faith in someone we have known.

When we meet such a person, who lives with what seems absolute trust, serene in the knowledge that "the Lord shall preserve you from all evil ... shall keep you safe," we tend to regard them with wonder. We may feel a secret envy, the longing to know such a rich relationship.

≈

How might you know God's care? Continually place yourself in God's care—when you wake from sleep, as you perform daily tasks, while you meet with others, when you eat your meals, before you go to sleep. Ask God to protect and guide you.

Psalm 122

I was glad when they said unto me,
"Let us go to the house of the Lord."

To read these lovely lines of hope while being aware of modern Jerusalem is to stretch credibility. The stone and glass towers echo the roar of traffic. The streets can erupt into violence without warning. The hatreds in the air are almost palpable. But I wonder if the city was very different at any other time in its long history, especially when a poet wrote these lines: "Peace be within your walls and quietness within your towers."

Great poetry often looks beyond immediate reality and sees something more hopeful and lovely, views a daunting situation and refuses to be defeated by it. To do this is to maintain that God makes possible—or that we, through God, can make possible—a better reality than what seems to be at present.

To have experienced the air of Jerusalem and the Middle East is to become aware of the tension all through this psalm. "Our feet are standing within your gates" conveys a sense of relief—the journey is always dangerous. "Jerusalem is … at unity with itself" sounds more like a wish or a prayer than a statement of actuality.

The "tribes of the Lord" can ignite into feuding at any moment. "Thrones of judgement" have always been necessary in this city—to keep the peace, to arbitrate ceaseless arguments. Even the repeated prayer for "peace," "quietness," and "prosperity" gives an indication of the fragility of the psalmist's society.

We ourselves live in such a society—nervous, watchful—its

fabric constantly tested by sudden events, its institutions under stress and tension in this time of transition. Yet we, like the psalmist, are called to live in the society of our own time as responsible believing men and women, thinking and speaking and acting hopefully, while at the same time praying for our own "Jerusalem," wherever it be and whatever its name.

In our own "Jerusalem"—our community, town, or city—it is our responsibility, as for the psalmist, to live "for my brethren and companions' sake" rather than merely for our own needs and purposes. It is our responsibility to "seek to do [our society] good."

꙰

Are peace and prosperity lacking in any sector of your community? Consider the power of continual and heartfelt prayer. Ask God to help all citizens realize their responsibility, and discover the strength and commitment to effect constructive change.

Psalm 123

*We have had more than enough of contempt ...
and of the derision of the proud.*

This is the second psalm that begins with the image of lifting up our eyes. In our society we very seldom have to lift our eyes when we deal with other people. We tend to look at one another directly. For the most part our meetings occur, as we say, on a level playing field.

Even when encounters are between someone who possesses power or influence and another who has some need—a conversation between an applicant seeking a job and an employer who has the power to decide—our culture encourages direct eye-to-eye contact.

Perhaps, therefore, we need the images in this psalm to remind us that there is One before whom we can fittingly lift up our eyes in reverence and, by implication, lower our eyes in humility. There is One to whom we can look "as the eyes of servants look to the hand of their masters, and the eyes of a maid to the hand of her mistress." That One is "the Lord our God."

We are not happy using such language to describe how we should behave. It smacks of subservience, and we feel ourselves to be free people. But reminding ourselves of our servanthood before God might help us appreciate the feelings of those who have to deal with the power we ourselves wield. Often we are surprised and hurt when other societies—or elements within our own society—are not grateful for what we see as our compassion and help.

Never having felt dependent ourselves, we find it difficult to understand how dependence can inculcate resentment and even rage. Toward the end of this psalm, strong emotion is vented. We are hearing a song of resentment against unjust power. There is agony in the lines, "We have had more than enough of contempt, Too much of the scorn of the indolent rich, and of the derision of the proud."

This ancient song sounds a warning. It is a timeless expression of the voice of poverty and oppression. We need to listen whenever the timeless theme of this psalm is sung in the pain and protests of our own time.

✍

Do you ever oppress yourself by judging yourself? Do you ever oppress others by judging them? Pray for all people oppressed by unfair judgement. Ask God to let compassion and understanding increase in the world, beginning in our own souls.

Psalm 124

We have escaped like a bird
from the snare of the fowler.

In Kenneth Branagh's production of Shakespeare's *Henry the Fifth*, there is a magnificently developed scene. The two armies have just fought a brutal and evenly matched battle. It is a grey day, pouring with rain. Everywhere are dead and dying men and horses. Some lie still, some move, some shriek in pain.

Through all this Henry walks alone. Across his face flit differing and fleeting expressions. He is exhausted, appalled, yet exuberant. He has won. But he is under no illusion that the outcome could have been different. He has discovered both weaknesses and strengths in his army and his tactics. He is wiser now.

Then he makes a decision. As we noted in the reflection on psalm 76, he orders that "Non Nobis," be sung. The anthem begins and gathers force. *Non nobis,* "not unto us." It is God who has given the victory.

This psalm shows us exactly such a moment. Obviously there has been a battle, and it has been won—but barely. "If the Lord had not been on our side ..." Twice the psalmist gasps out this conditional phrase. The idea of an alternative eventuality is almost unthinkable. It would have been absolute disaster. This enemy has certainly won the respect of the psalmist: "Then would they have swallowed us up alive."

A poem of war and victory snatched from defeat has something to say to us about our personal affairs and struggles. Notice how the poet-warrior describes the circumstances of himself and his fellows. They have "escaped like a bird from the snare of the fowler." They have discovered how vulnerable they are, in spite of their posturing and threats and battle cries. They have realized how much they depend on help beyond themselves.

We too have resources to do battle with life, personally and professionally—our skills, courage, experience, and tenacity. But if we are wise, we know that we are never completely self-sufficient. We need grace from beyond ourselves.

We bow our heads, sometimes experiencing exactly what the psalmist did—utter exhaustion and near surprise that we have survived the struggle—and we say, "Our help is in the name of the Lord."

❧

Recall an occasion when you were surprised by your own success. Could such an occasion in the past work to allay your fears and give you confidence in your success again in the future? Ask God to strengthen your confidence and rejuvenate your hope.

Psalm 125

The scepter of the wicked shall not hold sway
over the land allotted to the just.

Recently I was once again looking out over the Atlantic from the west coast of Ireland. As is almost always true in that part of the world, the west wind was bringing in a light rain, and the clouds were flying. I recalled how this coast and this ocean called the Christians of the early centuries to their endless voyages, and I realized again how geography shapes spirituality.

So too with the psalmist and those long-ago people. Two elements shaped their thinking—the rocky outcrop called Mount Zion, and the ascending approach to Jerusalem, which afforded its people some protection. An unexpected raid was almost impossible.

The psalmist tells us again that "those who trust in the Lord are like Mount Zion … The hills stand about Jerusalem; so does the Lord stand round about his people." Both these changeless realities—the mountain and the hills—remain a timeless metaphor for the people's deep trust in God.

But there is an implied warning in this psalm. It takes more than advantageous geography to afford protection. Real strength in a society derives from the moral quality of its life, and such morality is shown primarily in the degree of justice available to all in the society. "The sceptre of the wicked shall not hold sway over the land allotted to the just."

When the psalmist goes on to speak of "those who are good

and … true of heart," we may be led to hear a self-righteous tone. But the psalmist is not claiming that his society is good or true of heart. Instead, he is making a direct connection—both in the public and private sense—between the moral life of his society and its capacity to remain healthy and strong. The psalmist and many of his contemporaries knew this connection to be true in their time.

In spite of much change, much discovery, and much human achievement, the same is no less true in our time.

≈

Recall some occasions when the actions of your society have been "good and true of heart." How have these actions contributed to the strength and health of your society? Pray that the citizens and leaders of all nations may be "good and true of heart."

Psalm 126

The Lord has done great things for us,
and we are glad indeed.

Nothing in life is perhaps so wonderful as to long for something and then receive it contrary to expectation—a totally unexpected gift, a recovery from illness or failure, a breakthrough in a challenging situation. Such is the theme of this psalm.

Contrary to all expectation, some recent event has "restored the fortunes of Zion." The whole society is ecstatic. Given the realities of biblical times, the reason may have been success in battle, but it could equally have been a program of reform, or the signing of a treaty to ensure security.

Whatever happened, it was so unexpected that the people now seem "like those who dream." Obviously, the neighbouring countries are equally surprised because they too are saying, "The Lord has done great things for them [the Israelites]."

The psalmist describes the situation with a vivid image—the "watercourses of the Negev." At certain seasons of the year these watercourses are absolutely dry, without the slightest indication of ever flowing again. In fact, they may not flow for years. Then suddenly a rushing cascade will sweep all before it.

The psalmist now speaks of those "who go out weeping, carrying the seed ... [and who] come again with joy, shouldering their sheaves." Why such weeping and laughter? Because spreading the seed on such barren ground seems pointless. All the more joy and surprise when the seed produces a crop.

This psalm sings to us about the difference that can be made by our capacity for hope. In our society much looks barren, tears are more common than laughter. For many today, cynicism passes for sophistication.

But believing men and women are committed to the possibility that the future is always open to influences that can lead us in totally unexpected directions. In the language of the psalmist, we are called to be a people who believe that "the Lord [can do] great things for us."

❧

Recall a time when your lack of conviction caused you to doubt the possibility of your success. Consider how your attitude may have negatively influenced the outcome. Ask God to strengthen your trust in God, confidence in yourself, and hope for the future.

psalm 127

Unless the Lord builds the house,
their labour is in vain who build it.

as our society moves through its current phase of massive change, one of the many questions people are asking concerns the nature and meaning of work. People are demanding more and more that, whatever work they do, it must have meaning.

When the psalmist says, "It is in vain that you rise so early and go to bed so late ... to eat the bread of toil," he is expressing our human need for meaningful work. He uses religious language, but many secular statements make the same demand.

When we ask, "Why am I doing this?" or we say, "My work must be more than this," we are echoing the psalmist. We are assuming that there must be an ultimate meaning and intention beyond the immediate functional purpose of our work. It must somehow give us a feeling of being part of something greater than ourselves.

When the psalmist says, "Unless the Lord watches over the city, in vain the watchman keeps his vigil," he is voicing the same concern about his society. Unless there is a sense of our life existing within the providence of God—that is, comprising more than the sum of its activities and policies—then our energy and sense of purpose wither.

When the psalmist declares, "Unless the Lord builds the house, their labour is in vain who build it," he is affirming the most necessary element in family formation, indeed, in the nurture of all relationships—an acknowledgement of the presence of God.

Later in the song, immediately after the psalmist warns against making work our ultimate value, he speaks of children as a heritage and gift. For the psalmist, children become the allies of a parent when he or she "contends with … enemies."

We live in a society different in myriad ways from that of the psalmist, but we can still hear in these verses a reminder that our human relationships, especially those closest to us, are of ultimate value in our lives. They are to be treasured and nourished. We neglect them to our great loss.

≈

Would you agree that there is meaning and purpose in all work? Consider your own work. What meaning and purpose has it for you? For your colleagues? For others you serve? Ask God to inspire all people to discover meaning and purpose in their work.

psalm 128

Happy are they all who fear the Lord ...
happiness and prosperity shall be yours.

There is a lovely tradition that lives in the increasingly few and remote areas of western Ireland where Gaelic is still spoken. All greetings there are exchanged in religious terms.

If two people meet on a road, for example, one will say in Gaelic, "God be with you," and the other will answer, "God and Mary be with you." Or if the first person says, "God and Mary be with you," the other will answer, "God and Mary and Patrick be with you." Always the reply goes one step further than the salute.

This psalm gives a similar greeting and blessing, but even more elaborate. It tries to cover all the bases. In the ancient Hebrew world, the great word of greeting was "shalom." We tend to translate it into English as "peace," but it means far more. One of the many connotations of "shalom" is the idea of unity. When we greet a person with "shalom," we are wishing that all the blessings of life may come together for them.

In these lines the psalmist sings of "shalom." May you find great reward in your work and "eat the fruit of your labour." May all go well in the life of your family. May you have a good marriage. May children from your loving be like "olive shoots round about your table."

The list of good wishes continues. The psalmist expresses the hope that people in his society will remain prosperous and peaceful. "May you see the prosperity of Jerusalem all the days of your life."

Then comes the wish for long life. "May you live to see your children's children." Finally, we hear the hope of every generation—that the world will find peace. "May peace be upon Israel."

Beautiful and timeless lines—but we do them less than justice if we neglect to mention a particular theme running through them. "Happy are they all who fear the Lord, and who follow in his ways!" And later in the song, "The man who fears the Lord shall thus indeed be blessed." For the psalmist, there is one absolute essential condition for life to be completely fulfilling. The absolute essential is God.

If only this could be so for us and our world today!

꙾

Consider asking a blessing for someone you know. Hold them in your mind and heart. Wish for them the highest and best. Ask God to bless and care for them. Consider asking a blessing for another person or group, or an animal or natural phenomenon.

Psalm 129

Greatly have they oppressed me …
but they have not prevailed against me.

In the days before farm machinery, my grandfather on his farm in County Kilkenny could count on neighbours' help to reap his cornfields. The corn would be cut by mowing machine, but it would be gathered into sheaves and tied by people from nearby farms. My grandfather and my uncles and aunt would, in their turn, help on a neighbour's farm.

I can recall one rainy summer when the corn lay thin and light in our arms. Using an image of similarly poor grain, the psalmist dismisses those who have wronged and injured him and his people. "Let them be like grass [which] does not fill the hand of the reaper." Reminding me of my grandfather's instructions to clasp the corn to my chest before binding it, the psalmist speaks of the crop not filling "the bosom of him who binds the sheaves." This makes the image even more vivid.

"Let them [the enemies of Zion] be like grass upon the house-tops, which withers before it can be plucked." In those days in Israel—and until a generation ago in Ireland—one could some-times see grass growing on a roof. It never grew well, and no one would waste time gathering it. That is how the psalmist views his enemies—good for nothing, garbage to be swept away.

In a vivid image of the agony of being invaded and driven off the land, the psalmist sees the "plow" of an invader "plowing" not just the fields but the very backs of the dispossessed. His words,

"The plowmen plowed upon my back and made their furrows long," cry out with intense bitterness. This cry echoes in many parts of today's developing world where there seems no escape from exploitation and oppression.

The last verse of this psalm conveys the depth of scorn that the psalmist feels for his enemies. In his culture, saluting a fellow traveller on the road was considered a sacred obligation. To neglect such a salutation implied the deepest rejection possible. "Those who go by say not so much as, 'The Lord prosper you.' "

Obviously the oppression and ill treatment have gone on for a long time. "Since my youth," the psalmist says. Yet his spirit and his people's spirit have not been broken.

We have seen the like in recent history, when seemingly poor and backward societies have resisted powerful and sophisticated armies. Years later, after terrible suffering, when face-saving treaties have been made, the apparently backward people have been able to say, "Greatly have they oppressed me ... but they have not prevailed against me."

❧

Consider someone you know who has experienced severe hardship and has come through. What, in your view, enabled them to endure and triumph in the situation? Thank God for their example. Ask God to be with those who suffer hardship.

Psalm 130

My soul waits for the Lord
more than watchmen for the morning.

The Church of Saint Peter in Gallicantu—meaning cockcrow—stands on the steep slope of the Kidron Valley south of the walls of the old city of Jerusalem. To penetrate deep into its foundations is to enter a grim world of dungeons, where the official and sometimes brutal questioning of prisoners once took place.

At the deepest level is a pit carved out of the rock. The prisoner was lowered through a hole and left in darkness. Today beside this dreadful place a visitor will find a copy of this psalm. Nothing could more clearly convey the feeling of desolation that can occasionally sweep over the human soul.

"Out of the depths have I called you, O Lord; Lord, hear my voice." There is no hint of bargaining in this cry. The prisoner of darkness has nothing to bargain with. What we hear is utter supplication and pleading. There are moments in all human experience when we are such a prisoner.

In this psalm there is a hint of guilt also being involved. "There is forgiveness with you." Our own particular pit, however, may consist of sorrow, guilt, loneliness, or some other deeply painful burden.

There are situations in life when we can feel utterly helpless. All our personal resources are exhausted. At such times we realize that there is nothing to do but wait, hang in, survive. But wait for what, for whom? Not to have anything or anybody beyond oneself is to be totally bereft.

Our prayer is that we can be like the psalmist and "wait for the Lord." But even this waiting can have its terrors. "My soul waits for the Lord, more than watchmen for the morning," says the psalmist.

Such waiting is full of tension and fear. Every moment threatens. The darkness breeds enemies. The hours seem interminable. This is how the psalmist understands what it means to "wait for the Lord." He is not offering a shallow placebo. He repeats his determination to wait for the Lord no less than three times, precisely because waiting can sometimes require grim determination.

In reading this psalm we receive an utterly realistic insight about human experience. We are shown the depths we sometimes must experience—which others before us and around us have discovered to be deeper than the darkness—before we can taste "plenteous redemption."

❧

Have you known long waiting in a time of trouble? Consider establishing a pattern of daily prayer and meditation, and resting in the presence of God. Ask God to be with you. Let God share your trouble. Ask God to be with others who endure long waiting.

Psalm 131

I still my soul and make it quiet …
wait upon the Lord.

If a latter-day Alexis de Tocqueville had visited North America in the nineteen fifties and returned in the nineteen nineties, he would have been astonished at the return into everyday parlance of the term "spirituality." To his supremely observant mind it would have been obvious that a huge change had taken place in Western culture as it searched for its spiritual roots.

One mode of this search is what many have come to call "centering." There are many different understandings and different practices. Generally centering involves delving deep within the self, but the Christian will be searching for more than this. For beyond the self is that infinite centre-point, which the Book of Genesis describes as the "image of God" and St. Paul calls the "Christ within."

This psalm sings about such a search. "O Lord, I am not proud." This is not a priggish boast. It affirms that searching for the infinite centre is a far different enterprise from catering to the narrow self. The tyranny of selfish desire has been momentarily diminished.

"I do not occupy myself with great matters, or with things that are too hard for me." This is not an escape from the complexities and the challenges of life. It assumes a conscious reordering of priorities to make the centering process possible.

We move deeper into this process with the beautiful image of the "child upon its mother's breast." Again, this is not an unhealthy infantilism. It suggests choosing utter dependence on God as an antidote to the stress and anxiety of life. Notice the words, "I still my soul." Total dependence on God fosters an inner peace, which in turn enables our journey toward the presence of God. Every step is taken consciously and has a purpose.

"O Israel, wait upon the Lord, from this time forth for evermore." There is a hint of arriving at some point of discovery, some place where we might wish to stay for a long time. We are reminded of Peter wishing to stay on the mountain where his friend and Lord has been strangely transfigured.

Our personal prayer might be that we ourselves may experience such moments in our own efforts at centering.

꧂

Find about 20 minutes, quiet and alone. Sit comfortably. Breathe deeply. Relax from feet to head. Ask God to be with you. For up to 10 minutes repeat, silently or aloud, a suitable biblical phrase, such as, "Be still and know that I am God." Wait on God.

Psalm 132

I will surely bless her [Zion's] provisions,
and satisfy her poor with bread.

We are listening to a fascinating and complex human being make a fervent promise. His name is David. And he is extraordinarily gifted in many ways.

As a king, David can bring things into being by fiat, and he has just decided to build a temple for the God he passionately believes in. We catch this passion in his language. "I will not come under the roof of my house ... not allow my eyes to sleep ... Until I find a place for the Lord."

Now the scene changes. We hear excited voices. "The Ark ... we have it ... let us fall upon our knees before [God's] footstool." We are watching a procession carrying Israel's most precious object. Like the temple that David proposes, the ark is also a dwelling place for God.

Now both scenes fade. We are no longer concerned with temple or ark. We are in the presence of a people. "If your children keep my covenant," says God, "here will I dwell." Beyond mere constructed things, however beautiful and sacred they may be, is the presence of a living people dedicated to the living God.

"The Lord has chosen Zion," but not merely as a city of stone. For the rest of the psalm Zion takes on human characteristics. There is even a sexual quality in the words, "The Lord has chosen Zion, he has desired her for his habitation." As with any lover, God makes promises. "I will surely bless ... satisfy ... clothe ... [make her] rejoice and sing."

For us, this psalm joyfully recognizes the utter primacy of humanity in God's eyes. Temples may reflect the power of God—"A dwelling for the Mighty One of Jacob." The ark may be a rallying point—"let your faithful people sing with joy." But the ultimate allegiance and concern of God remains with the people themselves. For God, both the temple and ark are ultimately dispensable, but people, especially poor people, are not.

The psalmist has God say, "I will ... satisfy her poor with bread." Whenever and wherever the church lives out these priorities, her face becomes most like the face of God. When each one of us lives out these priorities, our state becomes most like our true state—children of God.

❧

Consider that God made the universe and dwells with it. Consider that God made you and dwells with you. Let yourself centre in this reality. Now consider that God made all living souls and dwells with them. How does this shape your attitude toward others?

Psalm 133

Oh, how good and pleasant it is,
… [to] live together in unity!

It would be fascinating to hear this psalm sung by the poet who wrote it. We might then be able to tell whether the first lines are an ecstatic celebration of unity that has just been achieved, or the expression of a deep longing for unity that remains elusive in spite of every attempt to achieve it.

"Oh, how good and pleasant it is, when brethren live together in unity!" We tend instinctively to interpret this line as an expression of longing. Unity is one thing we long for most in today's society, and one thing we find almost impossible to achieve.

The psalmist reaches for the most extravagant images to describe how intensely he longs for unity. For us today, these images may seem almost bizarre. But if we are ready to watch and feel and respond as he might, the images begin to make sense.

"It is like fine oil upon the head that runs down upon the beard … the beard of Aaron … the collar of his robe." Obviously, this image is crystal clear for the psalmist, as if he were a child watching something utterly incomprehensible yet marvellously fantastic and forbidden. He recalls a moment in the liturgies of his people when oil is poured on the priestly figure of Aaron, brother of the legendary Moses.

Rich and smooth and gleaming, the oil plasters the hair of the priest, glistens on his face, runs in rivulets down the furrows of his neck, and seeps into the material of his robe—and he doesn't care! He revels in the experience because he feels caressed, nourished, cleansed, and energized by the oil of God. This, suggests the psalmist, is what unity feels like among a people who discover it—utter ecstasy.

"It is like the dew of Hermon that falls upon the hills of Zion." The psalmist lives in north-eastern Galilee, up on what today is called the Golan, where the distant snow-capped peak of Mount Hermon forms a significant backdrop to people's lives, affecting their seasons and their crops, sending an early morning dew. This dew, like the flowing oil over Aaron, is the stuff of joy and hope and new life. And this too, sings the psalmist, is what it can be like to "live together in unity."

As we read him today, the psalmist calls us to strive for unity, to taste its elusive and hard-won sweetness, to come to know the energy it can release among us, and the blessings it can bring.

❧

Recall a situation where unity is lacking among the nations. Among your friends. In your family. In your own thoughts and feelings. Ask God to inspire you, your family, your friends, and all the nations to seek reconciliation, and to find the joy of unity.

Psalm 134

Behold now, bless the Lord, all you servants of the Lord,
you that stand ... in the house of the Lord.

Nothing more than a fragment—perhaps only a passing thought—
this psalm brings to mind those flashes of insight and reflection
we encounter in books like Blaise Pascal's *Pensées* or Dag Ham-
marskjöld's *Markings*. Often there is only a single idea, without
exploration or development.

Another instance is the note found in Pascal's jacket after he
died. "From about half past ten in the evening until about half past
midnight—Fire. Certitude. Feeling. Joy. Peace."

I have always thought of this psalm as addressing men and
women for whom worship and its sanctuaries have become dis-
tressingly familiar. I say "distressingly" out of concern for those
intimately and frequently involved in preparing, planning, and
leading public worship.

Those who study liturgy as a professional discipline—priests or
lay readers who lead worship, servers or altar guild members who
prepare the sanctuary for worship. Those who lead music ministries
of the church—organists, choir directors, choristers who spend
hours rehearsing, playing, and singing. Everyone of these people
frequently enters the sanctuary of God.

When they do so, their thoughts are focused on particular tasks
and duties—as they should be. But it is distressingly easy (and I
speak as a priest) to focus on the tasks so intensely that the mystery

and majesty of God—for whom the task is carried out and to whom the duty is offered—are altogether overlooked.

The psalmist speaks to "the servants of the Lord … that stand by night [or by day] in the house of the Lord." He tells them to "lift up your hands in the holy place and bless the Lord." And I hear these words being said to me.

The psalmist is telling me to make sure that, as I lead others in the words and actions of worship, I do not forget to offer worship myself. As I prepare the sanctuary for worship, I do not forget to prepare the inner sanctuary of myself. As I practise assiduously to perfect some piece of music, I do not become deaf to its beauty myself, or forgetful of the God to whose hearing it is offered.

Then, perhaps only then, will my duties and tasks "bless [me] out of Zion."

❧

When you perform an act of worship in a sacred place, an act of kindness for a living being, or an act of care for your own body and soul, dedicate your actions to God. Ask God to bless your actions that, through them, blessing may extend to all the world.

Psalm 135

Praise the Lord, for the Lord is good;
sing praises to his name, for it is lovely.

The great violinmaker, Stradivarius, was once heard to say, "God could not make Antonio Stradivari's violins without Antonio." Was that a moment of audacious arrogance or a wonderful expression of vocation? Perhaps there is always a thin line between regarding oneself as chosen and feeling oneself called to a particular task. In its writings, Israel appears at times on one side of the line, and at times on the other.

In this psalm we encounter a burst of impassioned praise for the God who has acted in history on behalf of his people. We learn why this God should be praised. "The Lord is good ... great ... above all gods." And we discover where this God may be found. "In heaven and on earth ... the seas and all the deeps ... lightning ... rain ... winds."

We hear what this God has done in the history of his people. God is the writer of the story of Israel. The psalmist tells us part of that story. "He overthrew many nations ... gave their land to be an inheritance ... for Israel his people." Is there an edge of callousness here? Do not other people matter to this great God?

Again, we hear that "the Lord gives his people justice and shows compassion to his servants." Is this justice for a particular people only? Is this compassion likewise limited?

The final verse gives us an idea of the mental map from which the psalmist speaks. "The Lord ... dwells in Jerusalem." Here is the kind of territorial thinking that the great mind and imagination of Isaiah challenges again and again. It is not wrong to feel chosen, so long as we understand that we are chosen to serve others. The moment we realize this, all arrogance vanishes and a sense of vocation takes over.

We twenty-first-century people need very much to feel chosen today. There are many reasons why we have lost a sense of being chosen by God. One reason is that we no longer regard history as the domain of God's presence and action. To recover a sense of being chosen to serve a God of history would help us to reclaim a sense of vocation to serve the world around us.

⍟

Consider the difference to your life if you could always recall that God pays special attention to you, and is intimately concerned and involved in everything you feel, think, and do. Pray that you may ever be mindful of God's infinite love and care for you.

Psalm 136

Give thanks to the God of gods ...
Who ... delivered us from our enemies.

Thanksgiving is a kind of therapy. Giving thanks for something underscores the fact that we have actually received it! We revel in the joy of possession. Being happy about anything is exceedingly good for us.

"Count your blessings," said various voices to us as children. This piece of handed-down wisdom is worth noting because, by counting our blessings, we bring a lot of positive energy into play within us.

This psalm was designed to arouse such positive energy in those who originally sang it. Being more about societal than personal blessings, it performs much the same function as a national anthem. It sets out to make the singers feel good about who they are as a people.

The psalm first reaches out to the whole of creation to paint a portrait of God. This God "by his wisdom made the heavens ... spread out the earth upon the waters ... created great lights ... sun ... moon ... stars."

Now the song turns nearer home and begins to tell the national story. In this story God is the one "who struck down the firstborn of Egypt ... brought out Israel ... divided the Red Sea ... made Israel to pass through the midst of it ... swept Pharaoh and his army into the Red Sea ... led his people through the wilderness

... struck down great kings ... gave away their lands for an inheritance [to Israel]."

A wonderful self-assurance is woven throughout this psalm. Today we envy such confidence in companionship with God. This psalm forces us to ask what we mean when we declare ourselves to be a people of God.

In this difficult and complex time, which many feel indicative of "our low estate," do we really believe that we have resources beyond ourselves? In this time when society faces serious threats to its stability, do we really believe that there is a source of strength to deliver us "from our enemies?"

What is the nature of these enemies? Are they within us as well as beyond us? To sing this psalm is to be challenged about our sense of who we are as a people.

❧

Consider an enemy currently threatening outside you. Consider an enemy inside you. What aspects of these threats are attributable to "physical causes?" What aspects are attributable to "spiritual causes"? Ask God for deliverance from such enemies.

Psalm 137

How shall we sing the Lord's song
upon an alien soil?

In Shakespearean tragedies we often watch a character change moods with astonishing rapidity. Someone will express deep depression or great sorrow with heartfelt eloquence. Then suddenly, without warning, the same person will convulse with rage. Sadness turns instantly to fierce anger. This is particularly true of Hamlet as he sweeps from one mood to another.

We witness the same kind of transformation in this song. The first line expresses utter sorrow; the last line, utter hatred. The song begins in tears and ends in blood.

The people of God are enduring bitter exile in Babylon. They gather in angry dispirited groups. Song has been silenced; dance has been stilled. "As for our harps, we hung them up on the trees." Those who have conquered them laughingly demand, "Sing us one of the songs of Zion." The reply of the psalmist haunts us in our own time. "How shall we sing the Lord's song upon an alien soil?"

Vast change is sweeping through Western society. Christians realize that the relationship between faith and culture will become increasingly different from what it has been in recent centuries. Much about Christian faith seems alien to many elements of contemporary society. As a result, many Christians feel that they live in a kind of exile from a remembered society.

This uncomfortable situation raises many questions about the ways that faith can be expressed, lived, and communicated in our culture. We might imagine contemporary voices asking the same question that was asked long ago by another people who felt themselves in exile. "How shall we sing the Lord's song upon an alien soil?"

From this place of exile and sorrow, the psalmist suddenly lashes out at the perceived enemy. "O Daughter of Babylon ... happy the one who pays you back for what you have done to us!" Although a perfectly understandable response, this would be a very bad recipe for Christian behaviour, even in perceived exile.

A much wiser course would be honestly to face those areas where Christian faith and witness have fallen short, to put effort into understanding contemporary culture, and to search for ways to communicate the faith in this culture.

≫

Consider the most pressing spiritual needs of contemporary culture. Consider your most pressing spiritual needs. Ask God to strengthen you and others in their search for God. May your search bring light to you and, through you, to others.

Psalm 138

When I called, you answered me ...
The Lord will make good his purpose for me.

In the first verse of this song, we receive a strong clue about the situation of the singer. He is giving thanks to God "before the gods." Probably he is in exile in Babylon, caught in what may be a huge pagan festival, with its many gods around him. Before, or in the face of, these gods he dares to praise the God of Israel.

Millennia later we share his situation. If the psalmist could travel in time and become aware of the gulf between faith and culture today, he would realize that the choice he had to make is also our choice. If "the gods" are those forces and values that powerfully call for our allegiance, then we are surrounded by the gods—economic, cultural, sexual, philosophical. We too can give thanks to God only if we are prepared to place God "before the gods."

"When I called, you answered me; you increased my strength within me." The psalmist has discovered the origin of faith. He trusts because God is a reality for him. At the end of the day, when all our theological arguing is over, personal experience is the basis for trust in God. When the leap of faith is made, it must be from this foundation.

This premise may sound simplistic. Some would argue that faith in God should be based on evidence far more concrete or intellectual. The truth is simpler, and it has been borne out in millions of lives by people who are prepared to say of God, "When I called, you answered me."

Such faith ventures to take one step more. On the basis of past experience in trusting God, it is prepared to trust God for the future. So the psalmist sings, "The Lord will make good his purpose for me."

To many of us, this kind of faith is enviable. Are we hearing only brave statements in the face of sometimes ghastly realities? A kind of determined whistling in the dark? This question is certainly valid. We can even detect a slight hint of anxiety in the psalmist's plea, "Lord … do not abandon the works of your hands," in other words, do not abandon me! The psalmist's vulnerability is showing, and we can identify with it.

Every single one of us lives on the boundary between trust and fear. We are all vulnerable. We do not have to be ashamed of this. It is our human condition. Faith offers the assurance that the God in whom we place our tentative and fragile trust will not finally betray us.

≈

Consider in what ways you are vulnerable. On whom or what do you depend for your physical needs? Your emotional needs? Your mental needs? Your spiritual needs? Ask God, many times every day, to guard and guide your body, feelings, mind, and spirit.

Psalm 139

Lord, you have searched me out and known me ...
where can I flee from your presence?

Even the most consistently exalted literature can sometimes excel itself. Suddenly we are presented with a passage that stands out from the surrounding greatness. In the body of the psalms, these verses offer such an encounter.

There are rare occasions when we feel that the unimaginable gulf between the divine and the human has, if only for a moment, been bridged and our humanity is actually addressing God. It may be that our human voice is expressing nothing more than a sense of utter humility—as in this psalm. Such a response may be all that is possible when our humanity stumbles into the presence of God.

"You have searched me out and known me ... you discern my thoughts ... You trace my journeys ... are acquainted with all my ways." There is nothing to do but bow the head in wonder and surrender. "Such knowledge is too wonderful for me."

Then begins the lovers' pursuit—the pretending to wish to flee, mingled with the longing to be seized and embraced. "Where can I flee from your presence ... to heaven ... the grave ... the sea ... the darkness?"

Everywhere love pursues and finds the fugitive, until the fugitive realizes that the pursuer is within him or her self, and always has been. "You knit me together in my mother's womb ... How deep I find your thoughts, O God!"

For the psalmist, it is inconceivable that all people may not share this passion for God. We hear a sudden surge of revulsion against such blindness. "Do I not loathe those who rise up against you?" Such vehemence appalls us. Perhaps realizing the darkness of what he is expressing, the psalmist makes an almost immediate self-correction. "O God ... try me and know my restless thoughts ... Look well ... lead me."

This passionate singer may realize that our allegiance to God is not measured by our alienation from those who believe otherwise, or may not believe at all. Quite the opposite. The quality of our relationship to God may best be measured by the quality of our relationships with those around us who tell a different story and take a different journey.

❧

God knows our inmost being. Searching our inmost being is one way to approach God. Consider implications of the truth that everyone's experience of God is different. Pray that people of different beliefs may share their experience and respect each other.

Psalm 140

Keep me, O Lord, from the hands of the wicked …
I have said to the Lord, "You are my God."

We are listening to someone who is under great stress. The very first lines of the psalm are a kind of terrified gasp for help in the face of some deeply dreaded threat. "Deliver me, O Lord … protect me from the violent."

People who have seen armed combat know how shattering it is to realize that someone remote and unseen is shooting with intent to kill you. These lines convey such sheer panic. "The violent … devise evil … stir up strife … are determined to trip me up." The psalmist feels totally trapped.

But something begins to steady him. He has made the discovery that he is not alone. "Listen, O Lord, to my supplication." He begins to realize that he possesses a source of strength other than his own: "O Lord God, the strength of my salvation."

Immediately on the heels of this prayer comes a fierce burst of antipathy toward those who threaten him. "Let the evil of their lips overwhelm them … Let hot burning coals fall upon them; let them be cast into the mire." When this vituperative urge is spent, the psalmist seems to relax, as if he feels the return of a sense of security, of being able to handle the situation. "I know that the Lord will … render justice to the needy."

This psalm points to an intriguing truth about the way human beings work. Anger can often be an antidote to fear. Anger can rally our inner forces when fear has deeply undermined them.

Often an angry response is triggered if our sense of justice—of the way things should be—is deeply offended. Something inside us screams, "This is not right! The deep down 'rightness' in things has been betrayed."

If we believe, as the psalmist does, that this rightness at the heart of things comes from God, then we can be moved to fight for it. We can be convinced that "the upright shall continue in [God's] sight." When this happens, we can stand rather than flee.

∾

Recall an occasion when your sense of fairness has been offended. Can you discover any of the "unfair" qualities in yourself? Be honest and gentle with yourself. Ask God to help you both accept the humanity and honour the goodness in yourself and others.

Psalm 141

My eyes are turned to you, Lord God ...
do not strip me of my life.

There is a special horror in the sudden awareness that we must get out of a situation largely of our own making. We realize how gentle and deceiving the slope of temptation has been. We admit, too, that we have rather enjoyed the process. But now we desperately want to stop and get off.

Such situations can occur in many areas of life, perhaps particularly in personal relationships and business life. All of them occur in this psalm.

First, the realization of what things have come to: "O Lord ... come to me quickly." Then, the recognition of saying things that have led to this trouble: "Set a watch before my mouth." Now, the understanding that our desire is obviously and utterly wrong: "Let not my heart incline to any evil thing." Next, the seeing of those around us as they really are: "Let me not be occupied ... with evildoers." And finally, the knowledge that we have already allowed ourselves to be seduced: "Let me not ... eat of their choice foods."

Now comes the wish for allies in the task of changing course: "Let the righteous smite me in friendly rebuke." We wish for a sympathetic voice, someone who has our welfare genuinely at heart, who will endorse our new intentions and strengthen our resolve. This is followed by the very uncomfortable acknowledgement that deep down we have always known the essential wrongness of the whole enterprise: "My prayer is continually against their wicked deeds."

Realization of all these things turns suddenly to revulsion: "Let their bones be scattered at the mouth of the grave." Now the moment of turning takes place: "My eyes are turned to you, Lord God." And for the first time the enormity of what has nearly happened becomes clear. There is panic in every phrase: "Do not strip me of my life. Protect me … from the traps." Followed by the final admission of utter dependence: "Let the wicked fall into their own nets, while I myself escape."

There is no neat ending. We do not know if there was a way out for the psalmist. But once again we have been given a stark picture of one aspect of our human nature.

~

Have you ever been in a "tight squeeze" of your own making? Is there something you now feel powerless to change? Ask God for guidance. Be open to the possibility that you may feel a desire to change. Pray that you may learn and follow God's will.

Psalm 142

When my spirit languishes within me,
you know my path.

"Nobody knows the trouble I'm in. Nobody knows but Jesus." The great spiritual songs of African American suffering come to mind when we read this psalm. These two poetic traditions—the psalm and the spiritual—exhibit similar patterns.

Both express suffering without reserve. There is no effort to hide tears, pain, and sometimes utter despair. Both cling to God as their final hope. Because of their trust in God, both traditions—Jewish and Black—display extraordinary depths of resilience. There is a capacity to survive and even triumph in the face of almost unimaginable suffering.

The psalmist beings with the words, "I cry." But there is more: "I cry to the Lord." The lamentation continues: "I make loud supplication." And again, "to the Lord." We can hear a contemporary counsellor advising a person in deep distress, earnestly encouraging them to "express" their sorrow or despair.

But this is not all that's going on here. The psalmist says, "I pour out my complaint before him [God]." Someone else is present, someone who cares, someone who can be trusted, someone of whom the psalmist can say, "You know my path."

The presence of another—for the psalmist, the Other is God—makes all the difference. The enemy that accompanies almost all suffering is the demon of loneliness—nobody understands my pain, my loss, my shame. The psalmist speaks for us all: "I look to my right hand and find no one who knows me; I have no place to flee to, and no one cares for me."

Yet always for the psalmist, there is God. We may shout at God, scold, blame, argue with, even accuse God. But God remains faithful. At the end of the day we too may cry, "You are my refuge, my portion in the land of the living."

The certainty that God stays constant, even when our humanity feels only the absence of God, is heard again and again in the psalms. The level of trust appears in the use of the simple word "when" in the last verse of this song. "When you have dealt bountifully with me," he sings.

For the psalmist, trust in God is a matter of "when" rather than "if." Such trust comes as a priceless gift to us.

≈

When you are in trouble, be sure to speak about the situation with someone you trust, often if necessary. Be sure to speak with God, many times a day. Seeking help is not a weakness but a strength. It takes courage to honestly share your situation.

Psalm 143

I spread out my hands to you;
my soul gasps to you like a thirsty land.

Toward the conclusion of director Oliver Stone's movie *Nixon,* the president approaches the end of his struggle against the many forces determined to unseat him. He is alone with the photographs of his predecessors, and in their company he breaks down and becomes emotional. His perceived enemies have won.

There is something of this moment in the experience of the psalmist. "My enemy has sought my life; he has crushed me to the ground; he has made me live in dark places like those who are long dead." Obviously, the situation has progressed beyond fear, beyond depression. This person is on the edge of disintegration. "My spirit faints within me; my heart within me is desolate."

The danger of getting into such a state is that we become incapable of reaching for help. Our "dis-ease" prevents us from reaching for what would assist us in our struggle. Here the psalms become an invaluable resource to the human spirit.

Even in the desolation that drains the spirit and thwarts action, the psalmist never loses the capacity to reach for God. He may be robbed of the power to hope, plan, or think clearly. He may feel surrounded by enemies and rendered totally helpless. Yet the voice of the psalms never hesitates to cry to the one source who can be trusted. "I spread out my hands to you; my soul gasps to you like a thirsty land."

We hear desperation in the plea, "Enter not into judgement

with your servant." When we are desperate, we know that our own weakness has played at least some part in the ghastly situation, but we do not want to hear that now. All we want is help, assurance, encouragement.

All of us know such moments. We admit that we have made mistakes. A sensitive friend or counsellor will refrain from speaking of such things. There may come a time to "enter into judgement," but now is not the time.

The gift of the psalms is to offer a repeated pattern in troubled circumstances. First, the unrestrained expression of despair. Then, the turning to God. Finally, a movement toward recovery and new resolve. The person who has been immobilized, "crushed … to the ground" is energized into action. "Show me the road that I must walk."

$$\approx$$

When you are in trouble, consult trusted friends or counsellors, and share repeatedly with God, be ready to listen for guidance—a word from a friend, a change in situation, a ray of intuition. God can choose to speak with us in many different ways.

Psalm 144

Rescue me ... from the hand of foreign peoples ...
whose right hand is raised in falsehood.

This psalm presents us with a vastly different mood from that of the preceding psalms. Although life is not ideal for the psalmist, we get the initial impression that he feels able to deal with it.

"Blessed be the Lord my rock!" The presence of God is deeply felt, strengthening and energizing the psalmist. God "trains my hands to fight and my fingers to battle." There is strong confidence in God. "My fortress, my stronghold and my deliverer, my shield."

But then we encounter a complete change of tone and mood, almost as if a shadow had passed over the spirit of the psalmist, a shadow kept at bay until this moment. "O Lord, what are we that you should care for us ... mere mortals ... We are like a puff of wind ... a passing shadow."

The psalmist has a sense of being threatened. Twice he mentions the source: "foreign peoples, Whose mouths speak deceitfully and whose right hand [the hand that communicates the wish for peace] is raised in falsehood."

We have no way of knowing whether the psalmist's fear is true or imagined, a projection on to people who are different. We do know that, as immigration patterns change, our own society can experience such feelings.

Like many people, the psalmist fears a threat to his way of life. His wishes for the future suggest this. "May our sons be like plants well nurtured … our daughters like sculptured corners of a palace … our barns be filled to overflowing … flocks in our pastures increase … our cattle be fat and sleek."

Our language would be different but might express the same hopes. May our children be successful and beautiful! May their place in the future changing society not be threatened! Is this not a reasonable expression of much contemporary hoping?

In the last moment of the psalm, we get a hint of the psalmist's presenting fear. "May there be no breaching of the walls, no going into exile, no wailing." At some previous time, perhaps in childhood, he has experienced the agony of invasion and conflict.

We realize that we have heard a very human voice poised between self-confidence and insecurity. For this reason we hear ourselves as we recite these lines.

✎

How do you react to people who are significantly different from you—in conviction, status, gender, race, or any other attribute? Consider some people and examine your feelings. Ask God to help you regard all people as souls on their journey to God.

Psalm 145

I will exalt you, O God my King,
and bless your name for ever and ever.

There are many psalms of praise, but the quality of these verses is different from most. In the poetry of the psalms almost every thought or feeling is expressed vehemently and passionately. But these lines seem calmer, as if the writer has found a place of peaceful tranquility that has prompted a meditative soliloquy on God, instead of a sustained burst of praise.

"Every day will I bless you and praise your name for ever and ever … there is no end." The psalmist seems to be giving himself to a mood, not wanting to emerge from it. "One generation shall praise your works to another." He is captured by a sense of time. There are moments when this happens to all of us.

We may be at the seashore, on a mountainside, or in a worshipping throng on some significant occasion. Suddenly we become aware of the many generations before us that have watched this breathtaking scene, heard this thunder of waves, sung this particular hymn, recited this prayer, and we will see ourselves standing in that succession of souls. "One generation shall praise your works to another," sings the psalmist. "They shall speak of the might of your wondrous acts, and I will tell of your greatness."

The deity depicted in these verses is different from the God we encounter in many psalms. Certainly this God is powerful and great, but here power and greatness are displayed in terms of gentleness. "The Lord is gracious and full of compassion … of great kindness … loving to everyone … merciful in all his deeds … lifts up those who are bowed down … near to those who call … hears their cry and helps."

As the psalm closes, a more familiar portrait of God flashes before our eyes. "The Lord … destroys all the wicked." For the psalmist, the righteousness of God makes this reaction inevitable. It completes the portrait of a God who is merciful and loving, who "preserves all those who love him," but before whom we are accountable for our choices and our actions.

⸙

Identify situations in the world where gentleness might have powerful effects. Identify situations in your own life where gentleness might have powerful effects. Pray that a spirit of grace and gentleness may grow in the world, and bring souls into harmony.

Psalm 146

[The Lord] gives justice to those who are oppressed,
and food to those who hunger.

Not long after the Second World War, one of the first great American musicals, *Oklahoma,* crossed the Atlantic. It came to the city of London, battered and wearied by war. The shadow of that terrible battle still hung over the personal lives of many. The euphoria of victory had passed, and the hard work of recovery and reconstruction loomed ahead.

Suddenly there were lights blazing onto a huge stage, images of open spaces with golden corn, and young vibrant voices singing, "O what a beautiful morning." It electrified an older world and brought a surge of energy and hope. Perhaps some good things were possible after all.

Just like songs, Hebrew poetry never tires of linking the seeming miracles of nature with the events of history. If the desert of Sinai can blossom, then the desert of horrible events in human affairs can blossom too. For the psalmist, nature and history are different manifestations of the same creating God.

But in the domain of history and human events, people need to be realistic. A watchful agnosticism—not necessarily cynicism—is recommended toward those in power. "Put not your trust in rulers, nor in any child of earth." Rulers are still creatures—nothing less, nothing more—creatures of a God who has created them and all that exists.

The psalmist does not presume to tell those in authority what to do or how to behave. Instead, he attributes certain priorities to God. The Lord "gives justice to those who are oppressed, and food to those who hunger … sets the prisoners free … opens the eyes of the blind … lifts up those who are bowed down … cares for the stranger … sustains the orphan and widow." Rulers would be wise to reflect these priorities in their policies and decisions.

On reading this psalm we realize how deeply the poetry is grounded in reality, and how political all artistic creations—including scripture—can be.

⟢

Consider some people in power, in both the public and private sector. To what extent do their policies and decisions include the priorities of this psalm? Pray that all rulers may seek and serve the source of all power, and honour the creations of that source.

Psalm 147

[The Lord] heals the brokenhearted ...
He counts the number of the stars.

Sometimes we are startled to realize that many contemporary claims to newness are false. One of the marks of post-modernism is the juxtaposition of seemingly disparate objects, combining elements that seem to have nothing in common, to make a new reality.

We may pride ourselves that much contemporary art and media displays this particular feature. But we have only to read a psalm such as this to realize that at least one person, the psalmist, got there before us by some twenty-five centuries!

This particular song paints a word portrait of God, as the psalmist understands God. Let us look at the many elements of this portrait and set them out in their disparate variety. Who is this God? What is God like, that it is "pleasant ... to honour him with praise"?

This God rebuilds cities ("Jerusalem"), reintegrates a scattered people ("gathers the exiles of Israel"), responds to the suffering of an individual life ("heals the brokenhearted"), governs the unimaginable reaches of space ("counts the number of the stars").

This God reigns with implacable justice ("lifts up the lowly"), hands out judgements ("casts the wicked to the ground"), encompasses the planet earth ("covers the heavens with clouds and prepares rain for the earth ... makes grass to grow upon the mountains"), disregards power exercised merely for its own sake, even human power ("strength of a man"). But this God longs for relationships of trust and faithfulness.

The goodness of this God demands response from those who receive his goodness. The vehicle of this goodness is a mystery called the Word. This Word not only "speaks" creation into being: "God sends forth his word ... and the waters flow." The Word also speaks in the human mind and heart in "statutes" and "judgements."

Here is a portrait of God that uses every possible element known to human life. The God of the psalms is neither pre-modern, modern, nor post-modern. This God is eternal and infinite. "Hallelujah!"

≈

Make a list of the main characteristics of the creator of all things. This creator listens and speaks to all creatures. In what ways and through what media might God speak to you? Take time every day, in quiet moments and in active moments, to listen for God.

Psalm 148

Let them praise the name of the Lord ...
his splendour is over earth and heaven.

If cinematography had been invented before this psalm was written, we might have seen a magnificent video. It would have shown space shots borrowed from NASA: "Praise the Lord from the heavens." It would have ransacked the great paintings of the renaissance for majestic winged creatures: "Praise him, all you angels of his ... all his host." It would have hurtled into the solar system, "sun and moon," and on through the galaxy, "all you shining stars." It would even have sailed out to the great aerial oceans that were once thought to flow above the skies: "waters above the heavens."

Perhaps this is where a twenty-first-century video would stop. Apparently, everything has been shown. But not so for the psalmist, and not so for us. Within the deepest "earth" and beyond the farthest "heaven" lies the ultimate beauty and majesty of the One who "commanded, and they were created," who "gave them a law which shall not pass away."

Now we are captured by the roving camera again. This time we explore earth itself. We plunge into the ocean to encounter "sea-monsters and all deeps." We are swept through weather systems and climates, "fire and hail, snow and fog, tempestuous wind." Again we notice that all these things are more than mere phenomena of nature. They do not merely exist. They are all "doing [God's] will."

Now we climb "mountains and all hills." We walk through

groves of "fruit trees and all cedars." We run with "wild beasts and all cattle," shrink from "creeping things," and wonder at the grace of "wingèd birds."

Then suddenly we are in the human world, with its structures and institutions, "princes and all rulers of the world." Beyond them, never wholly prisoners of principalities and powers, are "young men and maidens, old and young together." Finally, our ears are thrilled by the combined song of all creation, singing not of its own glory, but of the God whose "splendour is over earth and heaven."

With poetry like this, no wonder the ancients believed that the stars sang! Maybe they do, and our ears need to be more attuned to them. Then indeed we would be "a people who are near [God]."

☞

Make a list of some created things that especially disclose the nature of God to you. Recall some of what God has "said" to you, communicated to you, through some of those things. Ask God to help people to listen for God, and to hear God, in creation.

Psalm 149

Let the praises of God be in their throat
and a two-edged sword in their hand.

It can be a shattering experience when a friend suddenly speaks or acts in a totally unexpected way. Everything is going fine; the talk and the laughter are good. Then, without warning, something breaks through—perhaps hurt, anger, resentment. We are at a loss how to react.

Sometimes this happens in certain parts of the Bible. We are lulled by our familiarity with the general territory. We feel at home. Then suddenly the world of the Bible discloses assumptions and attitudes totally foreign to us.

The psalm begins by welcoming us into joyful worship. "Sing to the Lord a new song … in the congregation of the faithful." Musical instruments are strumming wildly. Various people are dancing. There is a sense of a society at ease with itself, a sense of God and this people being very close.

Suddenly the music, the dance, the worship—all screech to a halt. There is the hiss of swords being drawn. The language is chilling. Words like "vengeance … punishment … chains … iron … judgement" scream out. The people around us are transformed into an army, a relentless force that sees the world in terms of allies and enemies, defeat or victory. They have absolute certainty that God is their ally.

We do not want to follow this example. Must we then refrain from singing this song? Or can we sing it while construing a different meaning, valid for us? At the heart of this psalm is a truth to remember.

If a people are "joyful in their king," that is, if they believe firmly in a God of history, and if this people has formed an essentially just society, one that "adorns the poor with victory," then such a society will be strong. It will not necessarily be a warlike society, a conquering society, but it will be strong, and it will last. Such can be for us the theme of this song.

List the attributes of the society that you would be happy to "sing" about. How would such a society treat its disadvantaged? How would it encourage its leaders? Ask God to help you and other citizens to pray and work for a society with vision and compassion.

Psalm 150

Let everything that has breath
praise the Lord.

To reflect on the meaning of this psalm is a contradiction in terms. These lines are less about meaning and reflection than about ecstasy and celebration.

This psalm calls a congregation to leap out of the pews and sing and dance in the aisles. It calls the choir to shout its collective head off, and the organist to pull out every stop on the instrument. Probably the psalm should be sung a sufficient number of times for everyone to drop from exhaustion!

A bit of exaggeration? Of course, at least with respect to what passes for celebration in most mainline Christian congregations on a Sunday morning. But it is quite possible to witness this scenario in various parts of the world, especially in many African churches.

This psalm is immensely important for the churches of our twenty-first-century Western world. It demands that we consider allowing a measure of pentecostal fervour into our worship. Even to speak of a "measure" of "fervour" is a contradiction, a nod to our cultural limitations. We cannot measure the effect of the spirit on an individual or a congregation. In trying to do so, we would be deafened by the spirit's laughter.

How very far beyond the domain of religion this psalm takes us. Yes, indeed, praise is to be given in God's "holy temple," but we are pushed far beyond these walls. God is to be praised also in the vast domain of creation, "in the firmament of [God's] power."

And more, God is to be praised in the great process of time and history, the whole context of God's "mighty acts" and "excellent greatness."

Last of all, after it seems that every order of life has been included, the psalmist gathers together the assembled throng—like a musical Noah inviting every creature into a vast ark of sound—and calls all creation to raise an almost unimaginable shout of praise. "Let everything that has breath praise the Lord.'"

❧

Recall the many wonderful things that bring you joy and fulfilment—beauty of nature, reward of achievement, support of friendship, delight of intimacy. Let your body, mind, soul, and spirit engage and enjoy life to the full. Thank and praise God.

▌Path Books
A LIGHT TO MY PATH

We hope that you have enjoyed reading this Path Book. For more information about Path Books, please visit our website at **www.pathbooks.com**. If you have comments or suggestions about Path Books, please write us at **publisher@pathbooks.com**.

Other Path Books

God With Us: The Companionship of Jesus in the Challenges of Life by *Herbert O'Driscoll*
In 33 perceptive meditations, Herbert O'Driscoll considers the challenges of being human, searches key events in the life of Jesus, and discovers new vitality and guidance for our living, showing us how the healing wisdom and power of Jesus' life can transform our own lives today.
1-55126-359-9 soft cover, 160 pp., $18.95

Living Scripture: The Guidance of God on the Journey of Life by *Herbert O'Driscoll*
Where can we find truly inspiring models of leadership, friendship, creativity, and humanity to guide and motivate us? Reflecting on 29 well-known biblical characters — including Moses, Bathsheba, Naomi, Pilate, and Jesus himself — O'Driscoll shows how their strivings to live wisely, fully, and joyfully have relevance for our lives today.
1-55126-436-6 soft cover, 155 pp., $18.95

Christ Wisdom: Spiritual Practice in the Beatitudes and the Lord's Prayer by *Christopher Page*
The Beatitudes and the Lord's Prayer offer us a profound challenge to live in intimate communion with God. This pastorally-oriented book aims to help us discover new insights in Jesus' teaching. Each chapter includes reflective questions and spiritual exercises to help integrate the teachings into everyday life.
1-55126-420-X soft cover, 160 pp., $16.95

Mark's Gospel: Awakening the Voice Within by *Christopher Page*
The words of Mark's gospel turn a searching light into the souls of its readers, enabling us to examine our hearts, question our assumptions, and seek God's truth in our lives. Taking these words seriously, Page proposes, will change our lives in deep ways. Includes questions for journalling or discussion.
1-55126-450-1 soft cover, 184 pp., $19.95

Sacred Simplicities: Seeing the Miracles in Our Lives by *Lori Knutson*
In these engaging, two-page stories, Knutson shares her experience of the divine in the everyday, helping us to see glimpses of God where we least expect them. Enrichment for time at home or on the road, meditations with nature, or sermon illustrations.
1-55126-419-6 soft cover, 160 pp., $18.95

Available from your local bookstore or
Anglican Book Centre, phone 1-800-268-1168
or email abc@national.anglican.ca
or write 80 Hayden Street, Toronto, ON M4Y 3G2.